HBJ TREASURY OF LITERATURE

LIKE A THOUSAND
DIAMONDS

SENIOR AUTHORS
ROGER C. FARR
DOROTHY S. STRICKLAND

AUTHORS
RICHARD F. ABRAHAMSON
ELLEN BOOTH CHURCH
BARBARA BOWEN COULTER
MARGARET A. GALLEGO
JUDITH L. IRVIN
KAREN KUTIPER
DONNA M. OGLE
TIMOTHY SHANAHAN
PATRICIA SMITH
JUNKO YOKOTA

SENIOR CONSULTANTS
BERNICE E. CULLINAN
W. DORSEY HAMMOND
ASA G. HILLIARD III

CONSULTANTS
ALONZO A. CRIM
ROLANDO R. HINOJOSA-SMITH
LEE BENNETT HOPKINS
ROBERT J. STERNBERG

HARCOURT BRACE & COMPANY
Orlando   Atlanta   Austin   Boston   San Francisco   Chicago   Dallas   New York
Toronto   London

ISBN 0-15-300422-3

7 8 9 10   048   96   95   94

Acknowledgments continue on page 335, which constitutes an extension of this copyright page.

Acknowledgments

For permission to reprint copyrighted material, grateful acknowledgment is made to the following sources:

Marc Bloom: "Training Room" by Marc Bloom. Published in *Sports Illustrated for Kids*, June 1989.

Crown Publishers, Inc.: Cover illustration from *Elaine, Mary Lewis, and the Frogs* by Heidi Chang. Copyright © 1988 by Heidi Chang.

Dillon Press, Inc.: *A Gift for Tía Rosa* by Karen T. Taha. Text © 1986 by Dillon Press, Inc.

Laura Fernandez: Cover illustration by Laura Fernandez from *Different Dragons* by Jean Little. Illustration copyright © 1986 by Laura Fernandez.

Four Winds Press, an imprint of Macmillan Publishing Company: Cover illustration by Margot Tomes from *Ty's One-man Band* by Mildred Pitts Walter. Illustration copyright © 1980 by Margot Tomes.

Friends of Henry's and Ramona's Neighborhood: "Henry Huggins' Neighborhood" map by Heather Johnson.

Harcourt Brace Jovanovich, Inc.: Cover illustration by Jane Dyer from *Picnic With Piggins* by Jane Yolen. Illustration copyright © 1988 by Jane Dyer. *Piggins* by Jane Yolen, illustrated by Jane Dyer. Text copyright © 1987 by Jane Yolen; illustrations copyright © 1987 by Jane Dyer. Pronunciation Key from *HBJ School Dictionary*, Third Edition. Text copyright © 1990 by Harcourt Brace Jovanovich, Inc.

HarperCollins Publishers: "Writers" from *Hey World, Here I Am!* by Jean Little. Text copyright © 1986 by Jean Little. *Through Grandpa's Eyes* by Patricia MacLachlan. Text copyright © 1980 by Patricia MacLachlan. Cover illustration by Pat Cummings from *Storm in the Night* by Mary Stolz. Illustration copyright © 1988 by Pat Cummings. "People" from *All that Sunlight* by Charlotte Zolotow. Text copyright © 1967 by Charlotte Zolotow.

HarperCollins Publishers Ltd.: "Paddington" illustrations by Peggy Fortnum from *Paddington* books by Michael Bond.

Felice Holman: "Who Am I?" from *At the Top of My Voice and Other Poems* by Felice Holman. Text copyright © 1970 by Felice Holman. Published by Charles Scribner's Sons, 1970.

Henry Holt and Company, Inc.: Cover illustration by Ted Rand from *Knots on a Counting Rope* by Bill Martin Jr. and John Archambault. Illustration copyright © 1987 by Ted Rand.

Houghton Mifflin Company: From "Paddington Paints a Picture" in *Paddington on Stage* by Michael Bond and Alfred Bradley. Text copyright © 1974 by Alfred Bradley and Michael Bond. Based on the play *The Adventures of Paddington Bear*, published by Samuel French Ltd. All rights reserved. Cover illustration from *A River Dream* by Allen Say. Copyright © 1988 by Allen Say. *The Lost Lake* by Allen Say. Copyright © 1989 by Allen Say. Cover illustration by Lynn Munsinger from *Hugh Pine and the Good Place* by Janwillem van de Wetering. Illustration copyright © 1986 by Lynn Munsinger.

International Creative Management, Inc.: "Lisa's Fingerprints" from *Fingers Are Always Bringing Me News* by Mary O'Neill. Copyright © 1969 by Mary O'Neill.

Lothrop, Lee & Shepard Books, a division of William Morrow & Company, Inc.: From *Justin and the Best Biscuits in the World* (Retitled: "Spending Time with Grandpa") by Mildred Pitts Walter. Text copyright © 1986 by Mildred Pitts Walter.

Macmillan Publishing Company: "Some People" from *Poems* by Rachel Field. Published by Macmillan Publishing Company, Inc., 1957.

William Morrow & Company, Inc.: Illustration by Louis Darling from *Ellen Tebbits* by Beverly Cleary. Copyright 1951, 1979 by Beverly Cleary. From "Ramona's Book Report" in *Ramona Quimby, Age 8* by Beverly Cleary, illustrated by Alan Tiegreen. Copyright © 1981 by Beverly Cleary. Cover illustration by Alan Tiegreen from *Ramona Forever* by Beverly Cleary. Illustration copyright © 1984 by William Morrow & Company, Inc. Illustrations by Alan Tiegreen from *The Ramona Quimby Diary* by Beverly Cleary. Illustrations copyright © 1984 by William Morrow & Company, Inc. Cover illustration by Sheila Hamanaka from *Class Clown* by Johanna Hurwitz. Illustration copyright © 1987 by Sheila Hamanaka. From *The Adventures of Ali Baba Bernstein* (Retitled: "The Gathering of the David Bernsteins") by Johanna Hurwitz. Text copyright © 1985 by Johanna Hurwitz. *Johnny Appleseed* by Steven Kellogg. Copyright © 1988 by Steven Kellogg. Cover illustration by Michael Conway from *Vinegar Pancakes and Vanishing Cream* by Bonnie Pryor. Illustration copyright © 1989 by Michael Conway.

Orchard Books, a division of Franklin Watts, Inc.: Cover illustration by Peter Catalanotto from *All I See* by Cynthia Rylant. Illustration copyright © 1988 by Peter Catalanotto.

Picture Book Studio: Cover illustration by Yoshi from *Magical Hands* by Marjorie Barker. Illustration © 1989 by Yoshi.

G. P. Putnam's Sons: *What the Mailman Brought* by Carolyn Craven, illustrated by Tomie dePaola. Text copyright © 1987 by Carolyn Craven; illustrations copyright © 1987 by Tomie dePaola. "The Secret Place" from *Tomie dePaola's Book of Poems* by Tomie dePaola. Copyright © 1988 by Tomie dePaola.

Random House, Inc.: From *Red Ribbon Rosie* (Retitled: "Field Day") by Jean Marzollo. Text copyright © 1988 by Jean Marzollo.

continued on page 335

Dear Reader,

Diamonds—they're colorful, they glitter, they sparkle, they shine. Each one is a little different, but they're all beautiful. In this book you will read about many people who come from many special places. You will discover the special sparkle that each person adds to our world.

Adding sparkle to the world is often not easy. But it is possible. The stories in this book tell about some people who have done just that. You'll meet an African American Olympic champion who shines because of her hard work. An Asian father and son will show you that each person in this world adds his or her own special sparkle. You'll meet Alice, whose grandfather came from Europe long ago. She wants to travel all over the world, but her grandfather says, "You must do something to make the world more beautiful." What special color will she add? You'll also experience the warm glow of the love and friendship between two Hispanic families.

We hope that *you* feel the warmth of making new friends in the stories you read. We hope you see faraway places glisten in the sun. We also hope that meeting these people and places will challenge you to do something to make the world "sparkle like a thousand diamonds."

Sincerely,
The Authors

C O N T E N T S

7

UNIT ONE

BEING·SPECIAL

People find all kinds of ways to be special. Wangari Maathai started a tree-planting movement in Kenya to save the country from becoming a desert. Jackie Joyner-Kersee, a champion athlete, showed the world that hard work and determination could make things happen. As you read the selections in this unit, think about the chances the world gives you to be special.

THEMES

IMPROVING THE WORLD
. . . .

BEING DIFFERENT
. . . .

PLAYING TO WIN
. . . .

CLASS CLOWN

by Johanna Hurwitz

Lucas is one of the smartest boys in Mrs. Hockaday's third-grade class. He is also the most unruly one. Lucas doesn't really want to be the class clown, but being good isn't fun or easy. CHILDREN'S CHOICE, *SLJ* BEST BOOKS OF THE YEAR

HBJ LIBRARY BOOK

THE HARE AND THE TORTOISE

by Caroline Castle

This fable tells about the famous race between the proud hare and the patient tortoise—a new version of an old story. CHILDREN'S CHOICE

STORM IN THE NIGHT
by Mary Stolz

When the lights go out during a thunderstorm, Thomas learns more about Grandfather and himself as he listens to stories about Grandfather's boyhood. TEACHERS' CHOICE, CORETTA SCOTT KING HONOR

KNOTS ON A COUNTING ROPE
by Bill Martin and John Archambault

Boy-Strength-of-Blue-Horses learns about his birth, his first horse, and an eventful horse race from his grandfather. He also learns a lot about life each time they talk. *SLJ* BEST BOOKS OF THE YEAR

OX-CART MAN
written by Donald Hall
illustrated by Barbara Cooney

The story and detailed art by Barbara Cooney re-create the scenery and setting of the New England countryside during the early 1800s. At a market in Portsmouth, a farmer trades the special handmade goods his family produced and the ox and cart he made to carry them.
CALDECOTT MEDAL,
SLJ BEST BOOKS OF THE
YEAR, ALA NOTABLE BOOK

IMPROVING THE WORLD

Do you recycle empty glass bottles or aluminum cans? Do you pick up litter at home or at school? If you do, you are helping to make the world more beautiful. Read the following three selections to see what the characters have done to improve their environments.

CONTENTS

Miss Rumphius

Story and Pictures by BARBARA COONEY

The Lupine Lady lives in a small house overlooking the sea. In between the rocks around her house grow blue and purple and rose-colored flowers. The Lupine Lady is little and old. But she has not always been that way. I know. She is my great-aunt, and she told me so.

AMERICAN BOOK AWARD

CHILDREN'S CHOICE

TEACHERS' CHOICE

Once upon a time she was a little girl named Alice, who lived in a city by the sea. From the front stoop she could see the wharves and the bristling masts of tall ships. Many years ago her grandfather had come to America on a large sailing ship.

Now he worked in the shop at the bottom of the house, making figureheads for the prows of ships, and carving Indians out of wood to put in front of cigar stores. For Alice's grandfather was an artist. He painted pictures, too, of sailing ships and places across the sea. When he was very busy, Alice helped him put in the skies.

In the evening Alice sat on her grandfather's knee and listened to his stories of faraway places. When he had finished, Alice would say, "When I grow up, I too will go to faraway places, and when I grow old, I too will live beside the sea."

"That is all very well, little Alice," said her grandfather, "but there is a third thing you must do."

"What is that?" asked Alice.

"You must do something to make the world more beautiful," said her grandfather.

"All right," said Alice. But she did not know what that could be.

In the meantime Alice got up and washed her face and ate porridge for breakfast. She went to school and came home and did her homework.

And pretty soon she was grown up.

Then my Great-aunt Alice set out to do the three things she had told her grandfather she was going to do. She left home and went to live in another city far from the sea and salt air. There she worked in a library, dusting books and keeping them from getting mixed up, and helping people find the ones they wanted. Some of the books told her about faraway places.

People called her Miss Rumphius now.

Sometimes she went to the conservatory in the middle of the park. When she stepped inside on a wintry day, the warm moist air wrapped itself around her, and the sweet smell of jasmine filled her nose.

"This is almost like a tropical isle," said Miss Rumphius. "But not quite."

So Miss Rumphius went to a real tropical island, where people kept cockatoos and monkeys as pets. She walked on long beaches, picking up beautiful shells. One day she met the Bapa Raja, king of a fishing village.

"You must be tired," he said. "Come into my house and rest."

So Miss Rumphius went in and met the Bapa Raja's wife. The Bapa Raja himself fetched a green coconut and cut a slice off the top so that Miss Rumphius could drink the coconut water inside. Before she left, the Bapa Raja gave her a beautiful mother-of-pearl shell on which he had painted a bird of paradise and the words, "You will always remain in my heart."

"You will always remain in mine too," said Miss Rumphius.

My great-aunt Miss Alice Rumphius climbed tall mountains where the snow never melted. She went through jungles and across deserts. She saw lions playing and kangaroos jumping. And everywhere she made friends she would never forget. Finally she came to the Land of the Lotus-Eaters, and there, getting off a camel, she hurt her back.

"What a foolish thing to do," said Miss Rumphius. "Well, I have certainly seen faraway places. Maybe it is time to find my place by the sea."

And it was, and she did.

From the porch of her new house Miss Rumphius watched the sun come up; she watched it cross the heavens and sparkle on the water; and she saw it set in glory in the evening. She started a little garden among the rocks that surrounded her house, and she planted a few flower seeds in the stony ground. Miss Rumphius was *almost* perfectly happy.

"But there is still one more thing I have to do," she said. "I have to do something to make the world more beautiful."

But what? "The world already is pretty nice," she thought, looking out over the ocean.

The next spring Miss Rumphius was not very well. Her back was bothering her again, and she had to stay in bed most of the time.

The flowers she had planted the summer before had come up and bloomed in spite of the stony ground. She could see them from her bedroom window, blue and purple and rose-colored.

"Lupines," said Miss Rumphius with satisfaction. "I have always loved lupines the best. I wish I could plant more seeds this summer so that I could have still more flowers next year."

But she was not able to.

After a hard winter spring came. Miss Rumphius was feeling much better. Now she could take walks again. One afternoon she started to go up and over the hill, where she had not been in a long time.

"I don't believe my eyes!" she cried when she got to the top. For there on the other side of the hill was a large patch of blue and purple and rose-colored lupines!

"It was the wind," she said as she knelt in delight. "It was the wind that brought the seeds from my garden here! And the birds must have helped!"

Then Miss Rumphius had a wonderful idea!

She hurried home and got out her seed catalogues. She sent off to the very best seed house for five bushels of lupine seed.

All that summer Miss Rumphius, her pockets full of seeds, wandered over fields and headlands, sowing lupines. She scattered seeds along the highways and down the country lanes. She flung handfuls of them around the schoolhouse and back of the church. She tossed them into hollows and along stone walls.

Her back didn't hurt her any more at all.

Now some people called her That Crazy Old Lady.

The next spring there were lupines everywhere. Fields and hillsides were covered with blue and purple and rose-colored flowers. They bloomed along the highways and down the lanes. Bright patches lay around the school-house and back of the church. Down in the hollows and along the stone walls grew the beautiful flowers.

Miss Rumphius had done the third, the most difficult thing of all!

My Great-aunt Alice, Miss Rumphius, is very old now. Her hair is very white. Every year there are more and more lupines. Now they call her the Lupine Lady. Sometimes my friends stand with me outside her gate, curious to see the old, old lady who planted the fields of lupines. When she invites us in, they come slowly. They think she is the oldest woman in the world. Often she tells us stories of faraway places.

28

"When I grow up," I tell her, "I too will go to faraway places and come home to live by the sea."

"That is all very well, little Alice," says my aunt, "but there is a third thing you must do."

"What is that?" I ask.

"You must do something to make the world more beautiful."

"All right," I say.

But I do not know yet

what that can be.

THINK IT OVER

1. How did Miss Rumphius complete each of the three things she set out to do?

2. What are some of the faraway places Miss Rumphius visited?

3. Which of Alice's three goals do you think was the hardest to reach? Tell why you think as you do.

4. Do you agree with Alice's grandfather that a person should do something to improve the world? Tell why you feel as you do.

WRITE

If you could do something to make the world more beautiful, what would it be? Write a journal entry telling how you would make the world a more beautiful place.

When I was building a house in Maine, I noticed that we had an abundance of lupines on our land. Where did they all come from, I wondered. One of the workmen said, "There's an old woman down in Christmas Cove who goes around throwing lupine seeds. That's why there are so many flowers." I thought that was a good "seed" for a story.

One day, I sat down and said I would write a fairy tale about a heroine who had to do three things, and the hardest was the third, sowing the lupine seeds. The rest of the story patches together things that happened to me or my family. The story starts off in Brooklyn, where I was born, and the travels are mine, though I took them later in my life. My great-grandfather did carve cigar-store Indians, and my grandfather did help him paint in the skies in his pictures. I have ridden on camels, but I don't like them. It's too hard to get on and off!

Knowing I was going to have lots of lupines in my story, the minute they began to bloom I started drawing and photographing them. I didn't finish the book until much later, after the flowers were gone, but at least I had the drawings and the photos to work with.

When I create a book, I always do the story first. I think it's important to have a good story. The pictures come after the story, like beads on a string.

$\mathcal{W}$ORDS
from the
AUTHOR
and
ILLUSTRATOR:
Barbara Cooney

AWARD-WINNING
AUTHOR AND
ILLUSTRATOR

A SEED IS A PROMISE

BY CLAIRE MERRILL

You know a lot about seeds.

When you eat an orange, you see little white seeds inside.

You've seen the seeds of other fruits, too—apples, pears, melons, grapes.

Have you eaten peas or lima beans for dinner? Peas and lima beans are seeds. They are the seeds of vegetables.

Have you ever bought flower seed packets in the store? Or fed grass seed to a pet bird?

Have you ever worn maple tree seeds on your nose? Or played tea party with the seeds of an oak tree?

Do you know where all these seeds come from? All seeds come from plants.

And in every seed there is a promise, the promise that a new plant will grow.

If you know what kind of plant a seed comes from, you know what it will grow into.

ILLUSTRATED BY ANDREA EBERBACH

A bean seed will grow into a bean plant. An orange seed will grow into an orange tree. But an orange seed will never grow into a lemon tree.

How are seeds made? Most seeds begin inside flowers. Look at the center part of the flower. This is called the pistil. At the bottom of the pistil there are tiny egg cells.

Now look at the parts around the pistil. These are the stamens. They make a yellow powder called pollen.

A grain of pollen must reach an egg cell to make a seed.

Some flowers use their own pollen to make seeds. But most flowers use the pollen of other flowers.

Bees and other insects carry pollen from flower to flower. Wind blows pollen through the air.

A grain of pollen lands on the pistil of a flower. The pollen grain grows a long tube down into the pistil and joins an egg cell. A seed begins.

Soon the flower starts to die. Its petals dry and fall. The flower dies, but inside the pistil new seeds are growing.

As the seeds grow, a pod or a fruit grows around them. The fruit protects the seeds. The fruit gets bigger and bigger. It gets riper and riper.

The fruit breaks open. The seeds are ready to start new plants.

Some seeds fall to the ground right next to the plant that made them.

Other seeds travel.

The seeds of violets and pansies shoot into the air.

Milkweed and dandelion seeds ride silken strands into the wind.

Some seeds have sturdy wings that let them glide on the wind or float on the water.

Some seeds travel with your help or even with your dog's. Their sharp little burrs hook on to clothing or fur.

Not all of these seeds will grow into plants. Many things may go wrong.

A seed may not land on good earth. It may land on a rock, or in your house. A hungry bird or squirrel may eat it.

But almost every seed starts out with a chance to grow. You can find out why.

Soak a lima bean in water overnight. In the morning, let your mother or father help you cut the seed in half.

Inside you will see a tiny baby plant.

There is a tiny baby plant curled up tight in every seed. This tiny plant can grow into a big plant.

And as long as the tiny plant stays alive, there is a chance that the seed can keep its promise—even after a very long time.

Here is a true story about some seeds that grew after a *very, very* long time.

One day in the cold north country of Canada a miner was digging in the frozen earth.

Deep down, he found some old animal burrows. Inside the burrows were some animal bones. Next to the bones were tiny seeds.

The miner took the bones and seeds. He showed them to some scientists.

The scientists found out that the bones were the bones of little animals called lemmings. The bones were very, very old.

Thousands and thousands of years ago, in prehistoric times, the lemmings must have stored the seeds for food.

Everyone wondered, could such old seeds still grow? Had the earth acted like the freezer in your refrigerator? Had it kept the seeds from spoiling?

The scientists put the seeds on special wet paper and waited.

Two days later, this is what they saw. Some of the seeds had kept their promise. They had sprouted after thousands and thousands of years.

In time the seeds grew into healthy plants. The plants grew flowers. The flowers made new seeds—each with a promise of its own.

THINK IT OVER

1. What did you learn about plants from the story?

2. In what ways is a seed like a promise?

WRITE

Plants have many parts. List all of the different parts you know. Then write a description of a flower, telling what each part does.

JOHNNY APPLESEED

A TALL TALE RETOLD AND ILLUSTRATED BY
STEVEN KELLOGG

John Chapman, who later became known as Johnny Appleseed, was born on September 26, 1774, when the apples on the trees surrounding his home in Leominster, Massachusetts, were as red as the autumn leaves.

John's first years were hard. His father left the family to fight in the Revolutionary War, and his mother and his baby brother both died before his second birthday.

By the time John turned six, his father had remarried and settled in Longmeadow, Massachusetts. Within a decade their little house was overflowing with ten more children.

Nearby was an apple orchard. Like most early American families, the Chapmans picked their apples in the fall, stored them in the cellar for winter eating, and used them to make sauces, cider, vinegar, and apple butter. John loved to watch spring blossoms slowly turn into the glowing fruit of autumn.

Watching the apples grow inspired in John a love
of all of nature. He often escaped from his boisterous
household to the tranquil woods. The animals sensed
his gentleness and trusted him.

As soon as John was old enough to leave home, he set out to explore the vast wilderness to the west. When he reached the Allegheny Mountains, he cleared a plot of land and planted a small orchard with the pouch of apple seeds he had carried with him.

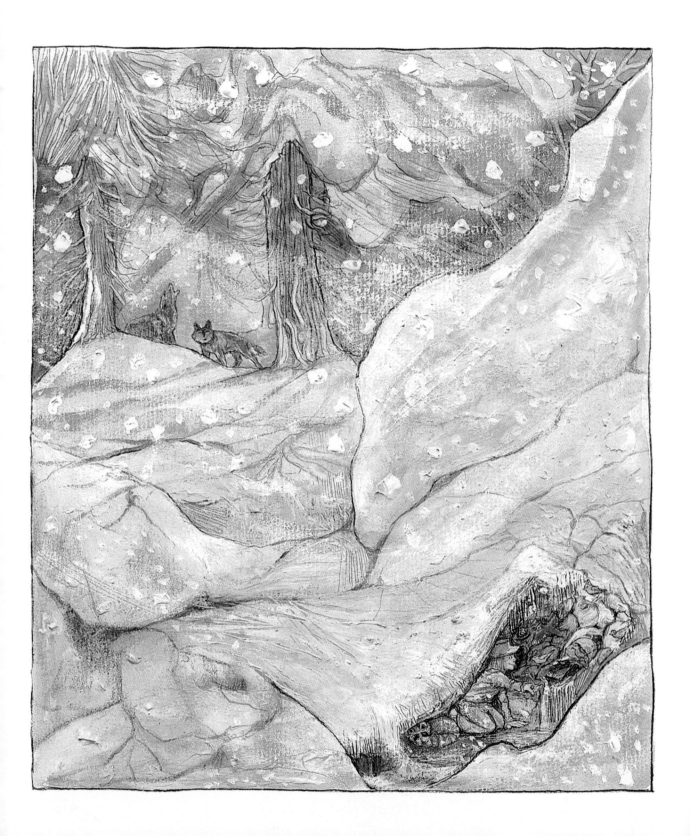

John walked hundreds of miles through the Pennsylvania forest, living like the Indians he befriended on the trail. As he traveled, he cleared the land for many more orchards. He was sure the pioneer families would be arriving before long, and he looked forward to supplying them with apple trees.

When a storm struck, he found shelter in a hollow log or built a lean-to. On clear nights he stretched out under the stars.

Over the next few years, John continued to visit and care for his new orchards. The winters slowed him down, but he survived happily on a diet of butternuts.

One spring he met a band of men who boasted that they could lick their weight in wildcats. They were amazed to hear that John wouldn't hurt an animal and had no use for a gun.

They challenged John to compete at wrestling, the favorite frontier sport. He suggested a more practical contest—a tree-chopping match. The woodsmen eagerly agreed.

When the sawdust settled, there was no question
about who had come out on top.

John was pleased that the land for his largest orchard had been so quickly cleared. He thanked the exhausted woodsmen for their help and began planting.

During the next few years, John continued to move westward. Whenever he ran out of apple seeds, he hiked to the eastern cider presses to replenish his supply. Before long, John's plantings were spread across the state of Ohio.

Meanwhile, pioneer families were arriving in search of homesites and farmland. John had located his orchards on the routes he thought they'd be traveling. As he had hoped, the settlers were eager to buy his young trees.

John went out of his way to lend a helping hand to his new neighbors. Often he would give his trees away. People affectionately called him Johnny Appleseed, and he began using that name.

He particularly enjoyed entertaining children with tales of his wilderness adventures.

In 1812 the British incited the Indians to join them in another war against the Americans. The settlers feared that Ohio would be invaded from Lake Erie.

It grieved Johnny that his friends were fighting each other. But when he saw the smoke of burning cabins, he ran through the night, shouting a warning at every door.

After the war, people urged Johnny to build a house and settle down. He replied that he lived like a king in his wilderness home, and he returned to the forest he loved.

During his long absences, folks enjoyed sharing
their recollections of Johnny. They retold his stories
and sometimes they even exaggerated them a bit.

Some recalled Johnny sleeping in a treetop hammock and chatting with the birds.

Others remembered that a rattlesnake had attacked his foot. Fortunately, Johnny's feet were as tough as elephant's hide, so the fangs didn't penetrate.

It was said that Johnny had once tended a wounded wolf and then kept him for a pet.

An old hunter swore he'd seen Johnny frolicking with a bear family.

The storytellers outdid each other with tall tales about his feats of survival in the untamed wilderness.

As the years passed, Ohio became too crowded for Johnny. He moved to the wilds of Indiana, where he continued to clear land for his orchards.

When the settlers began arriving, Johnny recognized some of the children who had listened to his stories. Now they had children of their own.

It made Johnny's old heart glad when they welcomed him as a beloved friend and asked to hear his tales again.

When Johnny passed seventy, it became difficult for him to keep up with his work. Then, in March of 1845, while trudging through a snowstorm near Fort Wayne, Indiana, he became ill for the first time in his life.

Johnny asked for shelter in a settler's cabin, and a few days later he died there.

Curiously, Johnny's stories continued to move westward without him. Folks maintained that they'd seen him in Illinois or that he'd greeted them in Missouri, Arkansas, or Texas. Others were certain that he'd planted trees on the slopes of the Rocky Mountains or in California's distant valleys.

Even today people still claim they've seen Johnny Appleseed.

THINK IT OVER

1. Why did people begin calling John Chapman by the name Johnny Appleseed?

2. Where did John get more apple seeds when he ran out of seeds to plant?

3. Johnny Appleseed learned to love all of nature by watching apples grow. What do you like to do that shows how you feel about nature?

WRITE

Think about what you learned about Johnny Appleseed. Then write a newspaper article telling about what you think is the most important event in his life.

IMPROVING THE WORLD

How do Johnny Appleseed and Miss Rumphius help make their worlds better?

. . . .

How does what you learned in "A Seed Is a Promise" help you understand how Miss Rumphius's seeds grew?

. . . .

WRITER'S WORKSHOP Miss Rumphius and Johnny Appleseed make some of their dreams come true. Think of a special goal that you want to reach. What steps would you follow to reach that goal? To help you get started, draw a diagram showing the steps leading to the goal as you see them. Share the information on the diagram with your classmates, and ask for their comments and suggestions. Then write a paragraph telling how to reach your goal.

53

54

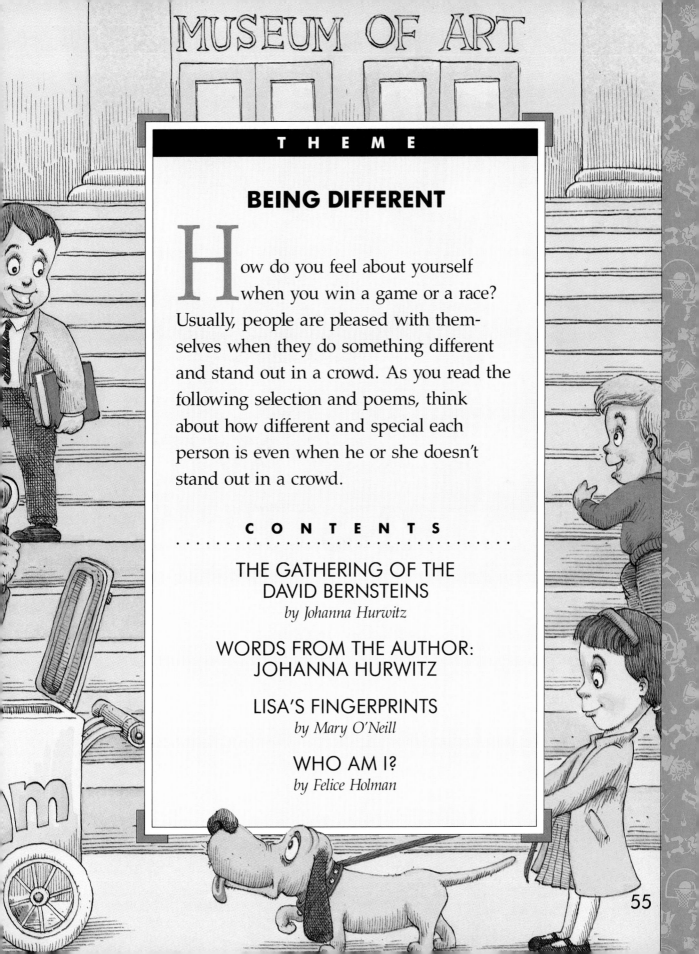

MUSEUM OF ART

BEING DIFFERENT

How do you feel about yourself when you win a game or a race? Usually, people are pleased with themselves when they do something different and stand out in a crowd. As you read the following selection and poems, think about how different and special each person is even when he or she doesn't stand out in a crowd.

CONTENTS

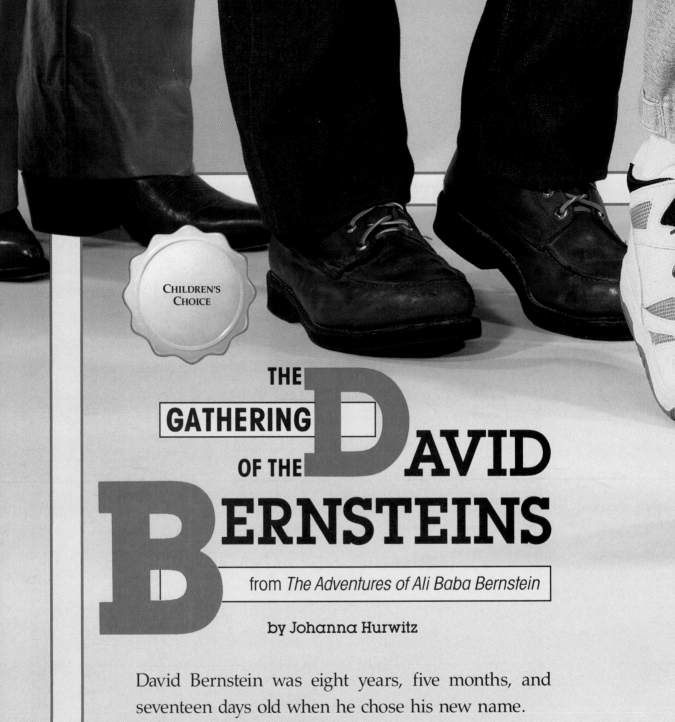

THE GATHERING OF THE DAVID BERNSTEINS

from *The Adventures of Ali Baba Bernstein*

by Johanna Hurwitz

David Bernstein was eight years, five months, and seventeen days old when he chose his new name.

There were already four Davids in David Bernstein's third-grade class. Every time his teacher, Mrs. Booxbaum, called, "David," all four boys

answered. David didn't like that one bit. He wished he had an exciting name like one of the explorers he learned about in social studies—Vasco Da Gama. Once he found two unusual names on a program his parents brought home from a concert—Zubin Mehta and Wolfgang Amadeus Mozart. Now these were names with pizzazz!

David Bernstein might have gone along forever being just another David if it had not been for the book report that his teacher assigned.

"I will give extra credit for fat books," Mrs. Booxbaum told the class.

She didn't realize that all of her students would try to outdo one another. That afternoon when the third grade went to the school library, everyone tried to find the fattest book.

Melanie found a book with eighty pages.

Sam found a book with ninety-seven pages.

Jeffrey found a book with one hundred nineteen pages.

David K. and David S. each took a copy of the same book. It had one hundred forty-five pages.

None of the books were long enough for David Bernstein. He looked at a few that had over one hundred pages. He found one that had two hundred fourteen pages. But he wanted a book that had more pages than the total of all the pages in all the books his classmates were reading. He wanted to be the best student in the class—even in the entire school.

That afternoon he asked his mother what the fattest book was. Mrs. Bernstein thought for a minute. "I guess that would have to be the Manhattan telephone book," she said.

David Bernstein rushed to get the phone book. He lifted it up and opened to the last page. When he saw that it had over 1,578 pages, he was delighted.

He knew that no student in the history of P.S. 35 had ever read such a fat book. Just think how much extra credit he would get! David took the book and began to read name after name after name. After turning through all the *A* pages, he skipped to the name Bernstein. He found the listing for his father, Robert Bernstein. There were fifteen of them. Then he counted the number of David Bernsteins in the telephone book. There were seventeen. There was also a woman named Davida and a man named Davis, but he didn't count them. Right at that moment, David Bernstein decided two things: he would change his name and he would find another book to read.

The next day David went back to the school library. He asked the librarian to help him pick out a very fat book. "But it must be very exciting, too," he told her.

"I know just the thing for you," said the librarian.

She handed David a thick book with a bright red cover. It was *The Arabian Nights.* It had only three hundred thirty-seven pages, but it looked a lot more interesting than the phone book. David checked the book out of the library and spent the entire evening reading it. When he showed the book to his teacher the next day, she was very pleased.

"That is a good book," she said. "David, you have made a fine choice."

It was at that moment that David Bernstein announced his new name. He had found it in the library book.

"From now on," David said, "I want to be called Ali Baba Bernstein."

Mrs. Booxbaum was surprised. David's parents were even more surprised. "David is a beautiful name," said his mother. "It was my grandfather's name."

"You can't just go around changing your name when you feel like it," his father said. "How will I ever know who I'm talking to?"

"You'll know it's still me," Ali Baba told his parents.

Mr. and Mrs. Bernstein finally agreed, although both of them frequently forgot and called their son David.

So now in Mrs. Booxbaum's class, there were three Davids and one Ali Baba. Ali Baba Bernstein was very happy. He was sure that a boy with an exciting name would have truly exciting adventures.

Only time would tell.

When Ali Baba Bernstein was eight years, eleven months, and four days old, his mother asked him how he wanted to celebrate his ninth birthday. He could take his friends to the bowling alley or to a movie. Or he could have a roller-skating party. None of these choices seemed very exciting to Ali Baba. Two boys in his class had already given bowling parties, another had invited all the boys in the class to a movie, and a third classmate was giving a roller-skating party next week. Ali Baba wanted to do something different.

"Do you remember when I counted all the David Bernsteins in the telephone book?"

Mrs. Bernstein nodded.

"I'd like to meet them all," said David. "I want to invite them here for my birthday."

"But you don't know them," his mother said. "And they are not your age."

"I want to see what they are all like," said Ali Baba. "If I can't invite them, then I don't want to have any party at all."

A week later, when Ali Baba was eight years, eleven months, and twelve days old, his mother asked about his birthday again.

"I told you what I decided," said Ali Baba.

That night Ali Baba's parents talked about the David Bernstein party. Mr. Bernstein liked his son's idea. He thought the other David Bernsteins might be curious to meet one another. So it was agreed that Ali Baba would have the party he wanted.

The very next morning, which was Saturday, Ali Baba and his father went to his father's office. Ali Baba had written an invitation to the David Bernstein party.

Dear David Bernstein:

I found your name in the Manhattan telephone book. My name is David Bernstein, too. I want to meet all the David Bernsteins in New York. I am having a party on Friday, May 12th at 7:00 P.M., and I hope you can come. My mother is cooking supper. She is a good cook.

Yours truly,
David Bernstein
(also known as Ali Baba Bernstein)
P.S. May 12th is my ninth birthday, but you don't have to bring a present.
RSVP: 211-3579

Mr. Bernstein had explained that RSVP was a French abbreviation that meant please tell me if you are going to come. He also said that his son should give his age in the letter.

"Honesty is the best policy, Ali Baba," his father advised.

Ali Baba was going to use the word processor in his father's office to print the letter. It took him a long time to type his letter on the machine. His father tried to help him, but he did not type very well either. When the letter was finally completed and the print button pushed, the machine produced seventeen perfect copies—one for each David Bernstein.

That evening Ali Baba addressed the seventeen envelopes so that the invitations could be mailed on Monday morning. His father supplied the stamps. By the end of the week, two David Bernsteins had already called to accept.

By the time Ali Baba Bernstein was eight years, eleven months, and twenty-nine days old, seven David Bernsteins had accepted his invitation. Four David Bernsteins called to say they couldn't come.

Six David Bernsteins did not answer at all.

Ali Baba and his mother chose the menu for his birthday dinner. There would be pot roast, corn (Ali Baba's favorite vegetable), rolls, applesauce, and salad. They were also having kasha varnishkas (a combination of buckwheat groats and noodles), which one of the guests had requested.

The evening of the party finally arrived. Ali Baba had decided to wear a pair of slacks, a sport jacket, and real dress shoes. It was not at all the way he would have dressed for a bowling party.

Ali Baba was surprised when the first guest arrived in a jogging suit and running shoes.

"How do you do," he said when Ali Baba opened the door. "I'm David Bernstein."

"Of course," said the birthday boy. "Call me Ali Baba."

Soon the living room was filled with David Bernsteins. They ranged in age from exactly nine years and three hours old to seventy-six years old (he was the David Bernstein who had asked for kasha varnishkas). There was a television director, a delicatessen owner, a mailman, an animal groomer, a dentist, a high-school teacher, and a writer. They all lived in Manhattan now, but they had been born in Brooklyn, the Bronx, Michigan, Poland, Germany, and South Africa. None of them had ever met any of the others before.

All of the guests enjoyed the dinner.

"David, will you please pass those delicious rolls," asked the mailman.

"Certainly, David," said the animal groomer on his left.

"David, would you please pass the pitcher of apple cider this way," asked the dentist.

"Here it is, David," said the television director.

"I have trouble remembering names," the seventy-six-year-old David Bernstein told Ali Baba. "At this party I can't possibly forget." He smiled at Ali Baba. "What did you say your nickname was?"

"Ali Baba is not a nickname. I have chosen it to be my real name. There are too many David Bernsteins. There were even more in the telephone book who didn't come tonight."

"I was the only David Bernstein to finish the New York City Marathon," said David Bernstein the dentist. He was the one wearing running shoes.

"The poodles I clip don't care what my name is," said David Bernstein the animal groomer.

"It's not what you're called but what you do that matters," said the seventy-six-year-old David Bernstein.

All of them agreed to that.

"I once read that in some places children are given temporary names. They call them 'milk names.' They can then choose whatever names they want when they get older," said David Bernstein the high-school teacher.

"I'd still choose David Bernstein," said David Bernstein the delicatessen owner. "Just because we all have the same name doesn't make us the same."

"You're right," agreed David Bernstein the mailman.

"Here, here," called out David Bernstein the television director. He raised his glass of apple cider. "A toast to the youngest David Bernstein in the room."

Everyone turned to Ali Baba. He was about to say that he didn't want to be called David. But somehow he didn't mind his name so much now that he had met all these other David Bernsteins. They *were* all different. There would never be another David Bernstein like himself. One of these days he might go back to calling himself David again. But not just now.

"Open your presents," called out David Bernstein the writer.

Even though he had said that they didn't have to, several guests had brought gifts. So after singing "Happy Birthday" and cutting into the ice-cream cake that was shaped like the Manhattan phone book, Ali Baba began to open the packages. There was a pocket calculator the size of a business card, just like the one his father had. There was a jigsaw puzzle that looked like a subway map of Manhattan, a model airplane kit, and a few books. One was a collection of Sherlock Holmes stories. "I used to call myself Sherlock Bernstein," the high-school teacher recalled. There was an atlas, and, best of all, there was *The Arabian Nights.*

"Now I have my own copy!" said Ali Baba. This was the best birthday he had ever had.

Finally, it was time for the guests to leave. "I never thought I would meet all the David Bernsteins," said David Bernstein the writer.

"You haven't," said Ali Baba. "Besides the seventeen David Bernsteins in the telephone book, there are six hundred eighty-three other Bernsteins listed between Aaron Bernstein and Zachary Bernstein. There must be members of their families who are named David. I bet there are thousands of David Bernsteins that I haven't met yet."

"You're right," said the seventy-six-year-old David Bernstein, patting Ali Baba on the back.

"Maybe I could invite them all next year," said Ali Baba. He was already nine years and six hours old.

"You could put an advertisement in the newspaper," suggested the mailman.

Ali Baba liked that idea.

David Bernstein the writer said, "I just might go home and write all about this. When did you get so interested in all the David Bernsteins?"

"It goes back a long time," said Ali Baba. "It all started on the day that I was eight years, five months, and seventeen days old."

THINK IT OVER

1. What is David's problem in this story? How does he solve it?

2. Why does Ali Baba put the letters *RSVP* on his invitation?

3. Why do you think the author has David read the telephone book?

4. How was David different at age 8 years, 11 months, and 4 days from when he was age 8 years, 5 months, and 17 days?

WRITE

Do you ever wish you had a different name or nickname? Write a paragraph explaining why you would or wouldn't change your name if you could.

Words from the Author:

Johanna Hurwitz

AWARD-WINNING AUTHOR

SUN PHOTO BY DAVID LIAM KYLE

AUTHOR! AUTHOR!
Johanna Hurwitz, writer of popular children's stories was a special guest at Berea's Fairwood Elementary School recently. "Busybody Nora," "Class Clown," "Rip-Roaring Russell," "Aldo Ice Cream," and others, portray everyday situations with humor and sympathy. Here, Ellie Gait, a fourth-grader, sits with Hurwitz as she speaks with students and signs autographs after several assemblies.

When I write a book, I seldom think of the title first. With *The Adventures of Ali Baba Bernstein*, it was the name that bounced into my head. I remembered that when my son was young, the name David was very popular, and at one time there were four Davids in his class. I decided to write about a boy who changes his name. I once wanted to change my name to Betsy, but now I like Johanna. When I was growing up, there were many girls named Joan and Joanne. Johanna is just different enough to make it special.

A Bronx Childhood Inspires Hurwitz

Johanna Hurwitz, children's book author

By MIRIAM RINN

The winner of many readers' choice awards, and with 30 books for children to her credit, Johanna Hurwitz once thought she'd never fulfill her childhood ambition to be a writer. Although she had been writing for a long time, the Long Island librarian kept getting flattering rejection notes and little else. Finally, her first book, "Busybody Nora," was taken on by Morrow Junior Books in 1975, and at the age of 38, Hurwitz was on her way. That book was

vited to speak to children from Texas to Alaska.

"I lived in the Bronx, and I never went anywhere," she says. "I read Laura Ingalls Wilder's "Little House" books, and I thought how much more interesting my life could be if we traveled across the country in a covered wagon and lived in a sod house," she recalls, laughing. "I never read a book that took place in the Bronx. Now I write my books that are set in the Bronx, or in a 20-mile radius from where I've lived all my life, and

no danger of abandonment or abuse. "I would like to think of a happier world," she admits. Today's children may also wish to inhabit such a world, Miss Hurwitz believes. She recalls meeting a

Sometimes I use things that happened to my children as a starting point for a story, but that's as close as I get to their lives. When my first book came out, they were 10 and 12, but the characters I was writing about, Busybody Nora and her brother, Teddy, were 5 and 3. What happened in the book was close to my family life, but because Nora and Teddy were so young, my children didn't feel as if I was talking about them, so they weren't self-conscious.

I always wanted to be a writer, but I never really knew I was a funny writer until after my first book was done. It surprised me. Sometimes I look at my stuff and say, "Hey, I wrote that! It's funny!" I guess the way I write fits in with my philosophy of life—you'd better laugh at things, or otherwise you'll be crying much of the time.

Lisa's Fingerprints

by Mary O'Neill

Some say I have my mother's nose,
My father's eyes, my uncle's toes,
And so I think it is just fine
My fingerprints are only mine.
Not my father, or my mother,
Or my sister or my brother,
Those now, before, or after me
Will lack this nonconformity.
No set of prints whose every line
Matches yours, or matches mine.
Is this distinction true within
The world of wing, paw, hoof, and fin?

Who Am I?

by Felice Holman
illustrated by Karen Barbour

The trees ask me,
And the sky,
And the sea asks me
Who am I?

The grass asks me,
And the sand,
And the rocks ask me
Who I am.

The wind tells me
At nightfall,
And the rain tells me
Someone small.

Someone small
Someone small
But a piece
of
it
all.

BEING DIFFERENT

How is Lisa like Ali Baba Bernstein?

· ·

If Ali Baba Bernstein had invited all the people listed in the telephone book with the name Ali Baba to his birthday party, how would his party have been different?

· ·

WRITER'S WORKSHOP   Write the newspaper article that David Bernstein the writer might write about the gathering. Remember to answer the *Who*, *What*, *When*, *Where*, and *Why* questions to be sure you include all the details.

77

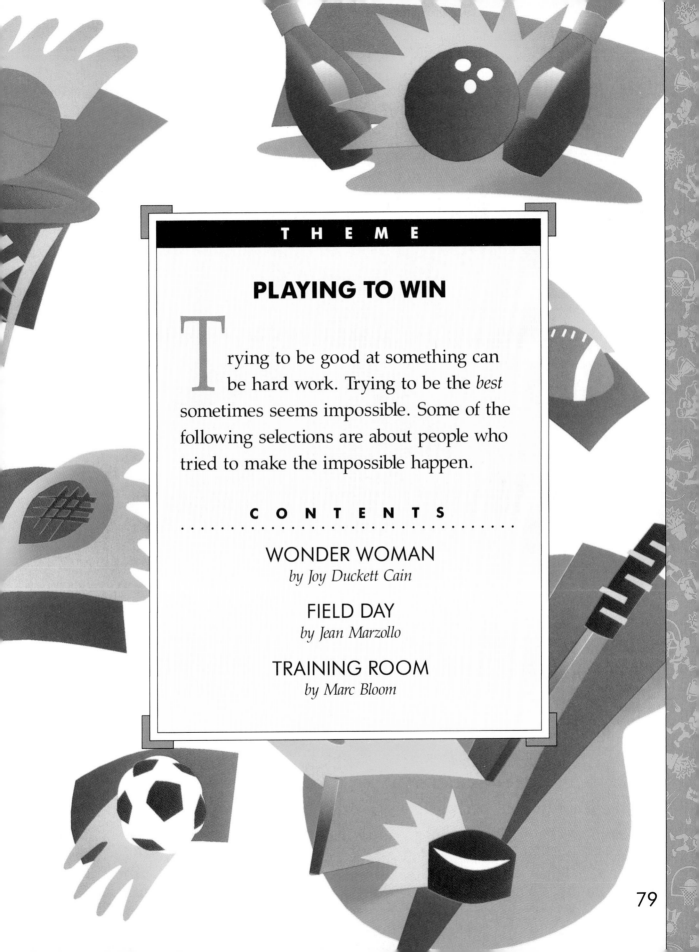

PLAYING TO WIN

Trying to be good at something can be hard work. Trying to be the *best* sometimes seems impossible. Some of the following selections are about people who tried to make the impossible happen.

CONTENTS

Wonder Woman

by Joy Duckett Cain ● • • • • • • • • • • • • • • • • •

WHEN JACKIE JOYNER-KERSEE was 10 years old, her 12-year-old brother, Al, bragged that he could beat her in a running race without even practicing. Jackie didn't think he could, and she began to practice every day.

On the day of the race, all of Al's friends were watching. He and Jackie ran from the mailbox at the corner of their street to the fence in front of their house, a distance of about 70 yards. The winner was . . . Jackie!

Fast and strong,
she's super-athlete
Jackie Joyner-Kersee!

LIGHT SPEED
Jackie Joyner-Kersee
can't outrun a
laser beam,
but she's fast as a flash
on the track.

"I felt kind of bad," Jackie says now. "I was a girl beating a boy, and Al's friends started calling him names. But by beating Al, I let him know I wasn't a pushbaround. And he learned to respect me as an athlete." Now, the whole world respects Jackie as an athlete. Many people think she is the best female athlete alive! That's because Jackie is more than just a fast runner. Her specialty is a track and field event called the heptathlon [hep-TATH-lon].

Jackie and Al have come a long way from their childhood home in East St. Louis, Illinois.

In the heptathlon, an athlete competes in *seven* different events. The events are (in order of competition): 100-meter hurdles race, shot put, high jump, 200-meter run, long jump, javelin throw, 800-meter run. Competitors earn points based on the times of their runs, the distances of their throws and the lengths or heights of their jumps. A heptathlon is held during two days. The person with the most points at the end of the second day is the winner.

Some people think that nobody on earth is better in the heptathlon than Jackie. She set the world record of 7,291 points at the 1988 Olympics while winning the heptathlon gold medal. Jackie has scored more than 7,000 points several times.

Jackie also won the 1988 Olympic gold medal in the regular long-jump competition. She set the American women's long-jump record with a jump of 24 feet 5½ inches. That is about the length of four beds placed end to end.

When Jackie was born in 1962, her great-grandmother Ollie Mae named her Jacqueline, after President John F. Kennedy's wife, Jacqueline. "Someday, this little girl is going to be the first lady of something," said Ollie Mae.

In 1988, Jackie was the first lady of track and field. But she

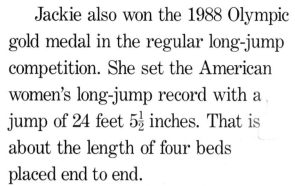

HIGH JUMP

800-METER RUN

THE HEPTATHLON
To excel in seven different events,
Jackie needs speed, strength and endurance.
She usually trains for five hours a day.

wasn't always a winner. In her first track meet, when she was 9, Jackie finished last in a 400-meter race. "I decided that this was a challenge and that I was going to do my best," says Jackie. "Now some of my friends who used to be better than me in track say 'Oh, I wish *I* had stayed in track!'"

Jackie grew up in East St. Louis, Illinois, which was a very poor community. She lived with her parents, her brother and her two younger sisters. Sometimes there was no heat in the house and very little food to eat. Still, Jackie didn't spend a lot of time worrying about the bad things in her life, because there were so many good things to do. Her parents insisted that she study hard and get good grades. Jackie became a cheerleader and a dancer. She even teamed up with her sisters and a bunch of friends to form a dance group. They called themselves the Fabulous Dolls.

One day, Jackie watched a television program about Babe Didrikson. Babe was an Olympic track and field champion in 1932, and she excelled in other sports. "Seeing Babe run the hurdles and play baseball, tennis and basketball was something!" Jackie says. "She was a very tough woman, and I admired her toughness."

100-METER HURDLES

85

JAVELIN

LONG JUMP

Jackie became more and more involved in sports. At Lincoln High School, she averaged 19.6 points per game as a senior forward on the girls' basketball team. She was captain of the volleyball team. She led her track team to three state titles and set the state record in the long jump. And she graduated near the top of her class.

Because Jackie excelled in sports and in the classroom, the University of California at Los Angeles (UCLA) gave her a basketball scholarship. For four years, Jackie started at forward for the women's basketball team and ran on the track team. She was named Most Valuable Player at least twice in each of those sports before she graduated in 1986.

200-METER RUN

SHOT PUT

These days, Jackie competes all over the world. Sometimes she competes in the heptathlon, and sometimes she enters single events such as her favorite, the long jump, or the 100- or 400-meter hurdles races. Jackie works hard to be the world's best athlete. Her coach, Bob Kersee, is also her husband. Jackie works out five days a week, and each workout is five hours long.

What is this super athlete like off the track? Jackie describes herself as "really wacky" and says that she likes to talk a lot. She also likes to play practical jokes. While she was growing up, her favorite targets were her brother and sisters. It's no wonder that Jackie's family nicknamed her the Joker.

Along with sports, there is something else Jackie takes seriously: helping kids. She remembers how some adults helped her when she was growing up. So, in 1988, she formed the Jackie Joyner-Kersee Community Foundation to help kids in East St. Louis. Jackie hopes the foundation can raise enough money to reopen the community center where she played sports as a kid.

Jackie also speaks to groups of kids at schools and clubs around the country. One of the things she talks about is what she has done to overcome asthma [AS-ma]. Asthma is a medical condition that makes breathing difficult, particularly during exercise. Jackie must take special medication every day so that she can breathe well enough to train hard.

Jackie is super-serious about her sport, but she can always find time for a quick run with some young fans.

Jackie is often asked about Florence Griffith Joyner, who earned three gold medals and one silver medal at the 1988 Olympics. Jackie and Flo-Jo are good friends. They are sisters-in-law, too, because Flo-Jo married Jackie's brother, Al, in 1987.

Jackie also talks about the 1984 Olympics in Los Angeles. She was favored to win the gold medal in the heptathlon, but she finished second to Glynis Nunn of Australia by a score of 6,390 to 6,385. You can't get much closer than that! If Jackie had run just one third of a second faster in the final event, the 800-meter run, she would have won.

When that heptathlon competition was over, Jackie felt very sad. But she felt very happy for someone else. Her brother, Al, had won the gold medal in the triple jump! Both Jackie and Al had come a long way from those childhood days when Jackie could outrun her brother on the streets of East St. Louis!

When Jackie talks to kids today, she usually tells them, "It's important to understand who you are and what it is that you want to do. Don't be afraid to be different."

When you think about all the different things that Jackie can do, how can you disagree?

THINK IT OVER

1. If you wanted to tell someone else about Jackie Joyner-Kersee, what would you say?

2. Why was winning her first race against her brother an important event in Jackie's life?

3. Jackie tells students not to be afraid of being different. What do you think she means by this?

WRITE

Pretend you are Jackie. Write three diary entries, each describing a different special day. In one of your entries, tell why winning the gold medal is important to you.

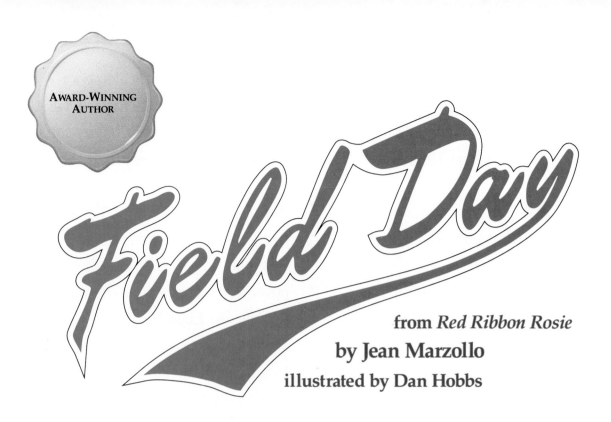

Field Day

from *Red Ribbon Rosie*
by Jean Marzollo
illustrated by Dan Hobbs

Rosie usually takes second place in the races
at school and receives a red ribbon. Her best friend,
Sally, always gets the first-place blue ribbon.

During a practice race for Field Day, Rosie tried to win
a race by not obeying all the rules. She lost—not only the
race but her best friend as well. To make things worse,
Sally will be on the opposite team during the Field
Day events.

When Rosie's sister, Jane, sees how upset Rosie is,
she comes to her rescue. Jane makes Field
Day costumes for Rosie's team for the
costume contest and assures her that
the team name is a good one.

On the big day, Sally's parents and
brother are friendly, but Sally isn't.

It was Friday, the big day. In the early morning the skies had been gray, but by eleven the sun had come out. Now it was shining on the third graders and their parents.

Sally still wasn't speaking to Rosie, but Sally's mom and dad and Ben waved hello. Ben flashed Rosie a *V* for victory sign, and Rosie flashed it back to him. She hoped the sign would bring her good luck.

Rosie needed all the luck she could get. She hated to have her best friend mad at her, and she felt bad that no one from her family was there to cheer for her team. Jane had said she might be able to come after high school was out. Her mother had said she might be able to come during her lunch hour. Her grandma had said she might come if she got her petunias planted. But that didn't add up to much.

The third graders stood in two separate lines. All the Ones wore red jerseys. All the Twos wore yellow jerseys. Rosie knew that her team wore red because they were the Fabulous Flying Fire Fish, but she didn't know what the yellow color stood for.

"May the best team win," said Mr. Mac. "And may both teams display good sportsmanship and have a good time. The winners of the name and costume contests will be announced after lunch. All I need to know now are the team names. Team One, what is your name?"

"The Fabulous Flying Fire Fish!" said Chris. Everyone cheered. It *was* a very good name, thought Rosie.

"Team Two," said Mr. Mac. "What is your name?"

"The Killer Bees!" said Sally. Everyone cheered again, and some of the Killer Bees buzzed. Killer Bees was a good name, too, thought Rosie.

"The sack race is the first event," said Mr. Mac. The Fabulous Flying Fire Fish and the Killer Bees went to the starting line and pulled up their sacks.

"Ready . . . on your mark . . . get set . . . go!" yelled Mr. Mac. Rosie hated the scratchy feel of the sack, but she tried to ignore it. She hopped faster than she ever had in practice. Soon she was ahead of everyone and halfway to the finish line! But then Billy, a Killer Bee, came up next to her. As Rosie tried to go faster, her feet got caught in the sack. She fell down. Billy won. Sally came in second.

One point went to the Killer Bees. The score was 1–0.

The next event was the three-legged race. Rosie's partner was Marco. They sat together on the starting line waiting for Mr. Mac to tie their ankles together.

"Remember, don't go too fast," said Rosie.

"I know," said Marco. "And start with your inside foot."

"I know," said Rosie.

Mr. Mac tied everyone's ankles together. When he was finished, he stood on the sideline and yelled, "Ready . . . on your mark . . . get set . . . go!"

Rosie started off with her inside foot, but Marco started with his outside foot. They tripped and fell down on the starting line.

"You used the wrong foot!" yelled Marco.

"I did not! You did!" cried Rosie.

They tried to get up, but they were both so upset that they fell down again. By the time they got going it was too late. The race was over. Sally and Sam had won.

Another point went to the Killer Bees. The score was 2–0.

The next event was the mystery toss. Mr. Mac held up something round and wet wrapped in a towel. "Guess what you're going to be tossing in the mystery toss," he said.

"Beach balls," said Billy.

"Marshmallows," said Chris.

"Balloons," said Rosie.

"Close," said Mr. Mac. Out of the bag he lifted a big, floppy balloon.

"Water balloons!" yelled Sally.

"Correct," said Mr. Mac.

"Yippee!" said Chris. "I hope it breaks and I get all wet. I need to cool off!"

"Some of you will definitely get wet," said Mr. Mac. "I promise. Now, stand facing your partner on the starting line."

The partners lined up. Rosie's partner, unfortunately, was Chris. "Chris," she pleaded. "I know you want to cool off, but please, throw the balloon gently. Let's try to win, okay?"

"Sure," said Chris.

Mr. Mac gave Rosie their water balloon. It was cold and wet and slippery. She had to hold it with both hands.

Mr. Mac blew his whistle. "Ready?" he said. "On your mark . . . get set . . . throw!" Rosie threw the heavy balloon to Chris very carefully. He caught it without breaking it and took one step backward.

"Good!" yelled Rosie.

Chris threw the water balloon back to Rosie. She caught it in her arms as gently as she could. It didn't break. So far so good. Rosie stepped backward, took a deep breath, and heaved the balloon. Chris caught it! He stepped backward and threw it back to Rosie. She caught it. They kept on this way. Each time they caught the balloon, one of them stepped backward.

Lots of other balloons down the line broke, and kids were shrieking as they got all wet. But Rosie and Chris were still dry. Rosie looked around. Sally and Freddy were still dry too. Soon Rosie and Chris and Sally and Freddy were the only four people left in the event. "We might win this!" Rosie yelled to Chris. "Pay attention!" She threw Chris the water balloon really carefully. He caught it and stepped backward. Now it was his turn to throw it to her.

"Here it comes!" yelled Chris. He threw the balloon way up in the air. It went higher than it had ever gone before. Rosie had her eyes right on it, and she knew she could catch it, but wasn't it coming down too fast? Could she catch it without breaking it?

Splat! The balloon hit her arms and burst open. Water splashed everywhere, and Rosie got soaked. Chris hooted with laughter.

Freddy threw his balloon to Sally, who caught it without breaking it. That was it. They had won the balloon toss. Rosie wished she had three giant water balloons to dump on Sally, Freddy, and her wonderful teammate Chris, who was still laughing.

One more point went to the Killer Bees. The score was now 3–zip.

Rosie sat in a patch of sunlight near the trees where the parents were serving lunch. She was wet and unhappy. The other kids were lining up for food, but Rosie didn't join them. The thought of hotdogs, pizza, popcorn, watermelon, and fruit punch made her feel sick. Nevertheless, after a while she went over and took a slice of pizza and a cup of punch. Then she went back to sit alone in her little patch of sun.

"Can I sit down too?" someone asked.

Rosie looked up. It was Sally. "I guess so," said Rosie.

Sally sat down with a grin. "I decided I'm not mad at you anymore," she said. "Isn't this fun?"

Rosie pretended she couldn't talk because her mouth was full.

"I said, isn't this fun?"

Rosie swallowed. Then she looked straight at Sally and said, "It's fun for you because you always win."

Sally's smile faded. She got up and said, "Forget I ever came over to talk to you."

Rosie felt worse than ever now, but she had to get up and join her team. It was time to put on the costumes. The costumes were in grocery bags at the side of the field. As Rosie unpacked them, everyone said the fins looked neat. Then her team helped each other put them on. Rosie thought the fins looked good too, but she still felt terrible.

Across the grass the Killer Bees were putting on their costumes—big, floppy yellow paper wings and long yellow feelers. Rosie watched to see if Sally was looking at her, but Sally didn't glance over once.

When the teams were ready, Mr. Mac blew his whistle, and the parade began. Each team had to march single file past a panel of teachers.

The Killer Bees went first. They had wrapped black tape around their jerseys for bee stripes and painted black stripes on their faces. As they walked by the judges, they flapped their arms and buzzed.

"Their wings droop," said Chris. "They should have made them out of cloth and cardboard like us. But listen to them. Don't they sound great?"

"Too bad fish don't make noise," said Marco.

"But they do!" said Chris. "Listen." He started to chant, moving his fins in time to it. "Swish, swish, bubble, bubble. Swish, swish, bubble, bubble." Everyone else on the team copied him.

"Swish, swish, bubble, bubble" went the Fabulous Flying Fire Fish as they passed before the judges. Rosie made the fish noise, too, but her heart wasn't in it. She kept thinking about her fight with Sally.

When the parade was over, the leader of the teachers' panel stood up. "Both teams have great costumes this year," she said, "so it was very hard to reach a decision. However, we have decided that first prize for costumes goes to . . . the Fabulous Flying Fire Fish!" The Fire Fish jumped up and down with happiness. All except Rosie. She just jumped up and down.

The score was now 3 to 1.

Mr. Mac held up a box. "All the teachers voted this morning on the team names," he said. "They put their votes in this box. I have counted them and would like to announce that first prize goes to . . . the Fabulous Flying Fire Fish!" The Fire Fish jumped up and down with happiness again. All except Rosie.

The score was now 3–2.

"Next we come to the award for good sportsmanship," said Mr. Mac. "All morning the Killer Bees won. That was great for them but very hard on the other team. But the Flying Fish didn't quit or cheat. So the Sportsmanship Award goes to . . . the Fabulous Flying Fire Fish!"

For the third time in a row the Fire Fish jumped up and down. And this time, even though Rosie was still worried about Sally, she felt a small thrill of excitement. The score was now tied 3–3, and it was time for the big race.

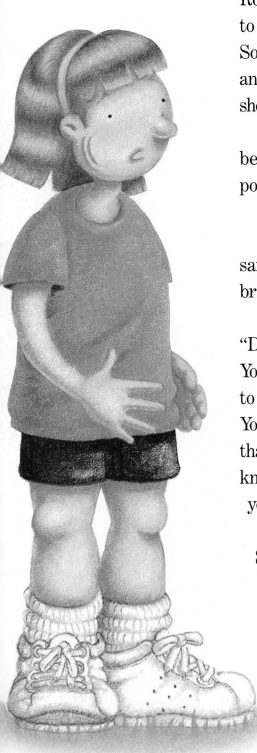

Rosie knew she had to do something
to save her friendship with Sally.
So she went up to the starting line
and stood next to her friend. "Hi,"
she said.

"Hi," said Sally. "Happy now
because your team won some
points?"

Rosie nodded. "Yes."

"Winning is fun, isn't it?"
said Sally. "What did you do—
bribe the teachers?"

"Oh, Sally, please," said Rosie.
"Don't be mad at me anymore.
You're my best friend, and I want
to wish you good luck in the race.
You'll probably beat me, and
that's okay. I just want you to
know that whatever happens,
you're still my best friend."

"Really and truly?" asked
Sally.

"Really and truly," said Rosie.
"Then you're my best
friend too," said Sally with
a smile. "It's no fun being
mad at you. I hope you
run a good race too.
Good luck."

Rosie smiled. All her jitters disappeared. Now she felt peaceful and calm.

Mr. Mac blew his whistle. "Ready!" he shouted.

The ten runners got in position.

"On your mark."

They got down.

"Get set."

They got up on their toes.

"Go!"

Off went the ten runners. They all got a good start because they were all good racers. Sally and Rosie were together at first, but then Sally pulled ahead. Rosie watched her best friend with mixed feelings. She was happy that she and Sally were friends again, but the truth was that she was also a little disappointed to see her friend winning.

"The most important thing is to enjoy a race," Ben had said. And it was true, Rosie did love to run. She loved it even now, with all her mixed feelings.

Ben had also said to concentrate and save your energy as if it were money. Rosie was running fast, but she wasn't running her very fastest. Sam and Sally were in front of her. Maybe one of them was spending too much energy.

Rosie put on just a little more speed. As she did, she came up next to Sam.

Up ahead was Sally.

I might be able to catch up with her, thought Rosie, starting to go a little bit faster. Far ahead she could see the finish line, where people were cheering.

Rosie heard a voice rise out from the crowd. "Come on, Rosie!" It was Jane yelling. "You're doing fine! Pour it on!"

Rosie started to run faster. She passed Sam on the homestretch. Sally was just a little bit ahead of her. Rosie heard another voice. "Go, Rosie, go!" It was Grandma!

In a great burst of speed Rosie caught up with Sally. She could hear Sam behind her, but she didn't turn to look at him. Instead, she concentrated on winning. She

still had a little extra energy left because she hadn't spent it all earlier.

She and Sally were neck and neck.

"Go, Poodle! Go, Toodle!" cried another familiar voice. It was Ben, cheering for both girls.

"Give it all you've got!" yelled someone else. It was Rosie's mother!

Rosie pumped her legs harder and harder and harder. At the last moment she burst past Sally and won the race.

"HOORAY ROSIE!" yelled the Fabulous Flying Fire Fish. Jane ran up and slapped her high fives. Mr. Mac shouted, "Congratulations, Rosie!" Her mother and grandma were beaming with pride.

Rosie felt herself being lifted high into the air. Ben had swung her up to the sky in his strong arms. She felt absolutely terrific.

Then, just as Ben swung her down to the ground, Rosie thought of Sally. Where was she? Did she feel terrible? She had never lost a race before. Rosie looked around at all the smiling faces as her mother and grandma both gave her a kiss at the same time.

"Thanks," she said. "But excuse me for a minute."

Rosie found Sally off to the side of the crowd, having a drink of punch with her parents. Her mom had her arm around her, and her father was taking her photograph, but Sally didn't look very happy.

"Hey, Rosie!" cried Sally's mom. "Come on over and get in the picture!"

"Are you sure you want me?" asked Rosie.

"Of course I'm sure," said Sally's mom.

"Is Sally sure?" asked Rosie.

Sally's face broke into a little grin. "Sure, I'm sure," she said. "Congratulations."

Sally and Rosie put their arms around each other and said "Cheese" for the camera.

The award ceremony was about to begin. Rosie and Sally went over to where everyone was waiting under the trees.

Rosie sat down on the grass next to Sally. She felt wonderful. She had won a race, the Fabulous Flying Fire Fish had won Field Day, and best of all, she and Sally were friends again.

That night Rosie pinned her first-place ribbon up on her bulletin board. It was the prettiest color blue she had ever seen.

It was true blue.

THINK IT OVER

1. What is the most important lesson Rosie learns? Tell why you feel it is so important.

2. What color is Sally's team wearing on Field Day?

3. Is it hard to compete against a good friend in a game or another activity? Explain why you feel as you do.

4. Rosie gets help and encouragement from many people. Who do you think is the most helpful? Give your reasons for thinking as you do.

WRITE

Think about how Rosie would feel if she had finished in second place. Write a conversation that Rosie and Sally might have after the race. Remember to use quotation marks around the words of each speaker.

Training

TEST YOUR STRENGTH, THEN MAKE YOURSELF STRONGER WITH FOUR EASY-TO-DO EXERCISES

illustrated by
Karen Visser

HOW STRONG ARE you? No matter how you answer that question, you probably wish you were stronger.

Strength is an important part of most sports. Top athletes like Mark McGwire of the Oakland Athletics exercise to build strength because they know it helps them play better.

Most doctors agree that even young boys and girls can safely exercise to develop strength. What exercises should you do?

First, take the following test. Do each exercise as many times as you can.

Remember: Warm up and stretch before and after you exercise.

108

Room

by
Marc
Bloom

PULL-UPS

Hang from a bar with your arms straight and your palms facing away. Pull up until your chin is over the bar, then lower yourself until your arms are straight again.

PUSH-UPS

Lie face down on the floor. Place your hands beside your shoulders. Keeping your back and legs straight, push up until your arms are straight, then lower yourself back to the floor.

CURL-UPS

Lie on your back with your knees bent and your feet 12 inches from your bottom. Fold your arms across your chest. Sit up and touch elbows to thighs, then lower yourself to the floor.

According to the President's Council on Physical Fitness and Sports, boys ages 8 to 13 should be able to do 5 pull-ups, 25 push-ups and 45 curl-ups. Girls should be able to do 2 pull-ups, 15 push-ups and 40 curl-ups.

Plan to retake this test in a month. In the meantime, here are four exercises you can do to build strength.

Do each exercise as described, rest one minute, and then repeat it two more times. Do the exercises every other day.

Curl Up

109

Be sure to check with your parents before you begin.

MODIFIED PULL-UPS

Place a pole across the seats of two chairs. Lie between the chairs with your chest under the bar. Pull up to the bar 10 times, keeping your body straight.

CRAB WALK

Sit on the floor with your knees bent. Reach behind you and lift yourself up on your hands and feet. Walk forward five steps and backward five steps. Add two steps each week.

CURL-UPS

Start with 10 curl-ups (as described in the test). Add two curl-ups per week.

PUSH-UPS

Do half as many push-ups as you did in the test. If you can't do regular push-ups, then keep your knees on the floor when you push yourself up.

Remember: Strength is important, but it is only one part of what it takes to be a good athlete.

The best athletes study as hard as they play, because strong bodies work best with sharp minds.

THINK IT OVER

1. What is the most important thing you learned from this article?

2. What exercises have you done or would you like to do to build up your strength?

WRITE

Make up an exercise of your own. Write directions telling how to do it.

Crab Walk

110

PLAYING TO WIN

Rosie and Jackie have to overcome problems in order to succeed. Think about something that you do well now that was difficult for you when you first started. What problems did you have to overcome in order to succeed?

. . . .

What are some qualities that a hero should possess? Tell whether the characters in the selections you read possess these qualities.

. . . .

WRITER'S WORKSHOP Find out about a sports hero or heroine who interests you. Then write a research report about the person. Tell how he or she became interested in and trained for the particular sport. Include several interesting details about the sports figure in your report.

Before you begin, you may want to organize the information for your report on a chart.

CONNECTIONS

Wangari Maathai

PLANTING TREES IN KENYA

For Wangari Maathai [wan·gar′ē mə·tī′], being special has meant working to save the environment of her native land, the East African country of Kenya. In 1977 she founded the Green Belt Movement to plant trees and end *deforestation*—the clearing of forests—in Kenya. For years Kenyans had been cutting down trees to use for firewood and to clear space to plant crops. The land was turning into desert.

Under Maathai's direction, the Green Belt Movement, which is made up mainly of women, has planted ten million trees in Kenya. Maathai has won praise and awards around the world, and the Green Belt idea has spread to a dozen African nations.

■ Find out what people are doing in your area to save the environment. Share your findings and ideas with your classmates.

GREEN SOLUTIONS

With a partner, find out about an environmental problem in the world and what's being done about it. Organize your findings on a chart like this one, and give a report to your classmates.

People planting trees for the Green Belt Movement

Problem		Actions		Results
There is too much trash.	⇨	1. Environmental groups write to newspaper editors. 2. _____	⇨	1. Awareness of the problem grows. 2. _____

MAKING A DIFFERENCE

Find out more about Wangari Maathai or another special person, such as Mother Teresa, who has worked to make the world a better place. Write a short report on that person.

UNIT TWO

FRIENDSHIPS

We're not a bit the same and yet,
We're closer than most people get.
Jean Little

Some friends you see every day, and some friends you may never meet. But how can someone you have never met be a friend? Antonia Novello is a friend to everyone in the United States because she is the doctor in charge of our nation's public health program. Dr. Novello is a friend who cares about our health and well-being. What makes someone a friend? Think about this question as you read the next selections.

BOOKSHELF

ELAINE, MARY LEWIS, AND THE FROGS

by Heidi Chang

Elaine Chow is very unhappy after moving to a small town in Iowa, until she shares a new friendship and a science project with Mary Lewis, a girl very interested in frogs. Elaine's father teaches them both something about his hobby, which helps them with their project and becomes a symbol of their friendship.

HBJ LIBRARY BOOK

RAMONA FOREVER

by Beverly Cleary

This book tells about Ramona's other adventures in third grade, along with some very special surprises and discoveries.

CHILDREN'S CHOICE, *SLJ* BEST BOOKS OF THE YEAR

TY'S ONE-MAN BAND
by Mildred Pitts Walter

This original American folktale, created by the author, tells about a peg-legged man named Andro who entertains others as a one-man band. One summer he brings joy to a town through the music he makes. AWARD-WINNING AUTHOR

DIFFERENT DRAGONS
by Jean Little

Ben is uneasy about visiting his Aunt Rose. He is also nervous around animals, during thunderstorms, and with new people. When his aunt surprises him with a new friend and a big dog, Ben learns that he is not the only one who has fears. AWARD-WINNING AUTHOR

MAGICAL HANDS
by Marjorie Barker

This beautiful story tells how William makes the birthdays of his three friends very special days. Striking illustrations help to tell the story of true friendship.

SCHOOL DAYS

While growing up, people often have some funny experiences mixed in with their everyday school activities. You are going to read about a funny character and about the author who created her—Beverly Cleary.

CONTENTS

119

RAMONA'S Neighborhood

Beverly Cleary was born, attended school, and grew up in Oregon. This walking map of the northeast section of Portland, Oregon, identifies landmarks from some of her books. The places shown on the map were suggested by people who read books in the Henry and Ramona series and searched for clues in them that referred to Portland landmarks. When they found clues, they described what happened there. Even though Beverly Cleary's characters are fictional, Ramona's neighborhood is a real place.

MAP KEY

1 Henry, Beezus, and Ramona live on **Klickitat Street** *(Henry and Ribsy)*.

2 Ramona wrote all over *Big Steve*, the book Beezus borrowed from the "Glenwood Library," otherwise known as the **Hollywood Branch of the Multnomah County Library** *(Beezus and Ramona)*.

3 **Laurelhurst School,** where Ramona started the third grade at the "Cedarhurst Elementary School" *(Ramona and Her Father)*.

4 Ramona got her bridesmaid's dress for Aunt Bea's wedding at **Lloyd Center** *(Ramona Forever)*.

5 Ramona and her new boots were stuck in the mud in front of **Kienow's Supermarket** *(Ramona the Pest)*.

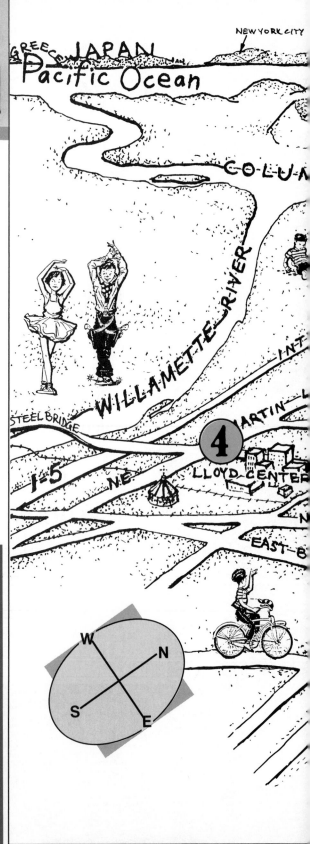

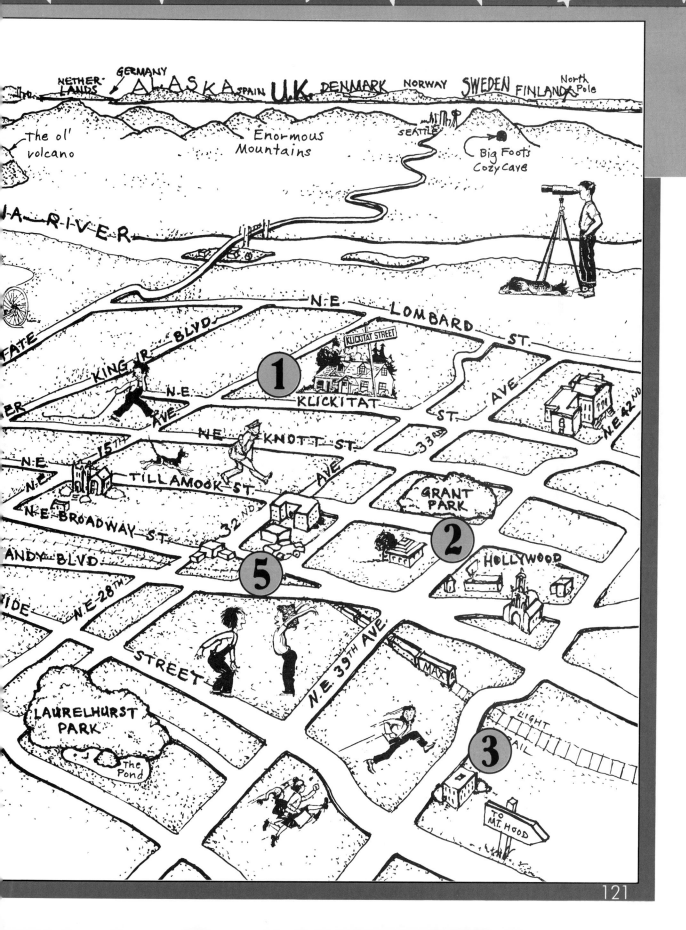

47350-0•**U.S. $3.25**
CAN. $4.50

A DELL YEARLING BOOK

A new school, a new start, and Ramona's set to go!

Beverly Cleary
Ramona Quimby, Age 8

A Newbery Honor Book

Ramona
enjoys third grade, but she
is often teased by a boy nicknamed
Yard Ape, and she thinks her teacher,
Mrs. Whaley, doesn't like her. When
Ramona breaks a raw egg instead of a boiled
egg on her head, she overhears Mrs. Whaley
calling her a show-off and really thinks of
herself as a nuisance.

After Ramona stays home from school
for a few days because she is sick, she
decides to begin working on a
book report.

RAMONA'S BOOK REPORT

from *Ramona Quimby, Age 8* **by Beverly Cleary**

illustrated by Alan Tiegreen

The book, *The Left-Behind Cat*, which Mrs. Whaley had sent home for Ramona to read for her report, was divided into chapters but used babyish words. The story was about a cat that was left behind when a family moved away and about its adventures with a dog, another cat, and some children before it finally found a home with a nice old couple who gave it a saucer of cream and named it Lefty because its left paw was white and because it had been left behind. Medium-boring, thought Ramona, good enough to pass the time on the bus, but not good enough to read during Sustained Silent Reading. Besides, cream cost too much to give to a cat. The most the old people would give a cat was half-and-half, she thought. Ramona required accuracy from books as well as from people.

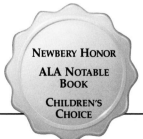

NEWBERY HONOR

ALA NOTABLE BOOK

CHILDREN'S CHOICE

"Daddy, how do you sell something?" Ramona interrupted her father, who was studying, even though she knew she should not. However, her need for an answer was urgent.

Mr. Quimby did not look up from his book. "You ought to know. You see enough commercials on television."

Ramona considered his answer. She had always looked upon commercials as entertainment, but now she thought about some of her favorites—the cats that danced back and forth, the dog that pushed away brand-X dog food with his paw, the man who ate a pizza, got indigestion, and groaned that he couldn't believe he ate the *whole* thing, the six horses that pulled the Wells Fargo bank's stagecoach across deserts and over mountains.

"Do you mean I should do a book report like a T.V. commercial?" Ramona asked.

"Why not?" Mr. Quimby answered in an absent-minded way.

"I don't want my teacher to say I'm a nuisance," said Ramona, needing assurance from a grown-up.

This time Mr. Quimby lifted his eyes from his book. "Look," he said, "she told you to pretend you're selling the book, so sell it. What better way than a T.V. commercial? You aren't being a nuisance if you do what your teacher asks." He looked at Ramona a moment and said, "Why do you worry she'd think you're a nuisance?"

Ramona stared at the carpet, wiggled her toes inside her shoes, and finally said, "I squeaked my shoes the first day of school."

"That's not being much of a nuisance," said Mr. Quimby.

"And when I got egg in my hair, Mrs. Whaley said I was a nuisance," confessed Ramona, "and then I threw up in school."

"But you didn't do those things on purpose," her father pointed out. "Now run along. I have studying to do."

Ramona thought this answer over. Well, Mrs. Whaley could just go jump in a lake, even though her teacher had written, without wasting words, that she missed her. Ramona was going to give her book report any way she wanted. So there, Mrs. Whaley.

Ramona went to her room and looked at her table, which the family called "Ramona's studio," because it was a clutter of crayons, different kinds of paper, tape, bits of yarn, and odds and ends that Ramona used for amusing herself. Then Ramona thought a moment, and suddenly, filled with inspiration, she went to work. She knew exactly what she wanted to do and set about doing it. She worked with paper, crayons, tape, and rubber bands. She worked so hard and with such pleasure that her cheeks grew pink. Nothing in the whole world felt as good as being able to make something from a sudden idea.

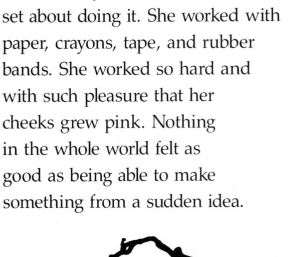

Finally, with a big sigh of relief, Ramona leaned back in her chair to admire her work: three cat masks with holes for eyes and mouths, masks that could be worn by hooking rubber bands over ears. But Ramona did not stop there. With pencil and paper, she began to write out what she would say. She was so full of ideas that she printed rather than waste time in cursive writing. Next she phoned Sara and Janet, keeping her voice low and trying not to giggle so she wouldn't disturb her father any more than necessary, and explained her plan to them. Both her friends giggled and agreed to take part in the book report. Ramona spent the rest of the evening memorizing what she was going to say.

The next morning on the bus and at school, no one even mentioned Ramona's throwing up. When school started, Ramona slipped cat masks to Sara and Janet, handed her written excuse for her absence to Mrs. Whaley, and waited for book reports to begin.

After arithmetic, Mrs. Whaley called on several people to come to the front of the room to pretend they were selling books to the class.

Then Mrs. Whaley said, "We have time for one more report before lunch. Who wants to be next?"

Ramona waved her hand, and Mrs. Whaley nodded.

Ramona beckoned to Sara and Janet, who giggled in an embarrassed way but joined Ramona, standing behind her and off to one side. All three girls slipped on their cat masks and giggled again. Ramona took a deep breath as Sara and Janet began to chant, "*Meow,* meow, meow, meow. *Meow,* meow, meow, meow," and danced back and forth like the cats they had seen in the cat-food commercial on television.

"*Left-Behind Cat* gives kids something to smile about," said Ramona in a loud clear voice, while her chorus meowed softly behind her. She wasn't sure that what she said was exactly true, but neither were the commercials that showed cats eating dry cat food without making any noise. "Kids who have tried *Left-Behind Cat* are all smiles, smiles, smiles. *Left-Behind Cat* is the book kids ask for by name. Kids can read it every day and thrive on it. The happiest kids read *Left-Behind Cat*. *Left-Behind Cat* contains cats, dogs, people—" Here Ramona caught sight of Yard Ape leaning back in his seat, grinning in the way that always flustered her. She could not help interrupting herself with a giggle, and after suppressing it she tried not to look at Yard Ape and to take up where she had left off. ". . . cats, dogs, people—" The giggle came back, and Ramona was lost. She could not remember what came next. ". . . cats, dogs, people," she repeated, trying to start and failing.

Mrs. Whaley and the class waited. Yard Ape grinned. Ramona's loyal chorus meowed and danced. This performance could not go on all morning. Ramona had to say something, anything to end the waiting, the meowing, her book report. She tried desperately to recall a cat-food commercial, any cat-food commercial, and could not. All she could remember was the man on

television who ate the pizza, and so she blurted out the only sentence she could think of, "I can't believe I read the *whole* thing!"

Mrs. Whaley's laugh rang out above the laughter of the class. Ramona felt her face turn red behind her mask, and her ears, visible to the class, turned red as well.

"Thank you, Ramona," said Mrs. Whaley. "That was most entertaining. Class, you are excused for lunch."

Ramona felt brave behind her cat mask. "Mrs. Whaley," she said, as the class pushed back chairs and gathered up lunch boxes, "that wasn't the way my report was supposed to end."

"Did you like the book?" asked Mrs. Whaley.

"Not really," confessed Ramona.

"Then I think it was a good way to end your report," said the teacher. "Asking the class to sell books they really don't like isn't fair, now that I stop to think about it. I was only trying to make book reports a little livelier."

Encouraged by this confession and still safe behind her mask, Ramona had the boldness to speak up. "Mrs. Whaley," she said with her heart pounding, "you told Mrs. Larson that I'm a nuisance, and I don't think I am."

Mrs. Whaley looked astonished. "When did I say that?"

"The day I got egg in my hair," said Ramona. "You called me a show-off and said I was a nuisance."

Mrs. Whaley frowned, thinking. "Why, Ramona, I can recall saying something about my little show-off, but I meant it affectionately, and I'm sure I never called you a nuisance."

"Yes, you did," insisted Ramona. "You said I was a show-off, and then you said, 'What a nuisance.'" Ramona could never forget those exact words.

Mrs. Whaley, who had looked worried, smiled in relief. "Oh, Ramona, you misunderstood," she said. "I meant that trying to wash egg out of your hair was a nuisance for Mrs. Larson. I didn't mean that you personally were a nuisance."

Ramona felt a little better, enough to come out from under her mask to say, "I wasn't showing off. I was just trying to crack an egg on my head like everyone else."

Mrs. Whaley's smile was mischievous. "Tell me, Ramona," she said, "don't you ever try to show off?"

Ramona was embarrassed. "Well . . . maybe . . . sometimes, a little," she admitted. Then she added positively, "But I wasn't showing off that day. How could I be showing off when I was doing what everyone else was doing?"

"You've convinced me," said Mrs. Whaley with a big smile. "Now run along and eat your lunch."

Ramona snatched up her lunch box and went jumping down the stairs to the cafeteria. She laughed to herself because she knew exactly what all the boys and girls from her class would say when they finished their lunches. She knew because she planned to say it herself. "I can't believe I ate the *whole* thing!"

THINK IT OVER

1. What did Ramona learn in this story? What did Mrs. Whaley learn?

2. Who gave Ramona the idea to advertise her book with a television commercial?

3. When did Ramona realize that Mrs. Whaley liked her?

4. What grade would you give Ramona on her book report? Explain why.

WRITE

If you had to present a book report as an advertisement, what kind of advertisement would you use? Choose a book you've enjoyed reading and write the advertisement you would use for it.

Writer Ilene Cooper spoke with Beverly Cleary to find out how she created the characters in her books. This interview tells where Ms. Cleary got the ideas for her characters. It also tells how Beverly Cleary became interested in reading and writing.

MS. COOPER: Ramona is so funny, and she comes up with all kinds of interesting ideas, such as the way she did her book report. Were you at all like Ramona when you were a child?

MS. CLEARY: I think I was like Ramona until I started school. I lived on a farm where I was wild and free and could use my imagination. I was allowed to do almost anything I wanted to do as long as it was safe. When I began school, I became much more like Ellen Tebbits, another character.

MS. COOPER: What did you do for fun when you were a child?

MS. CLEARY: When we moved from the farm, I lived in the kind of neighborhood that had front lawns and back lawns—not very big ones but we played there and on the sidewalk. We played a lot of sidewalk games: jump rope, jacks, hopscotch. We didn't go into one another's house unless we were invited by the mother. So we were all out on the street jumping around and yelling. We also played hide-and-seek and run-sheep-run. Some of the kids played soccer. But my mother wouldn't let me play because it was too hard on my shoes.

MS. COOPER: But you wanted to?

MS. CLEARY: Not much. I was not an athletic child. My idea of exercise was to sit in my child-size rocking chair with my feet propped up and read a book. If you're a reader then that's really what you want to be doing most of the time.

MS. COOPER: What did you like to read when you were a third and fourth grader?

MS. CLEARY: Well, I read the complete fairy tale section of our branch library. I did have a couple of favorite books when I was in the third and fourth grades—one favorite, but it's out of print now.

MS. COOPER: What was the name of it?

MS. CLEARY: *Dandelion Cottage* by Carol Rankin.

MS. COOPER: Did you always like to read?

MS. CLEARY: Oh, no.

MS. COOPER: But you made the change from somebody who didn't like to read to a reader— a real reader.

MS. CLEARY: Yes, in the third grade.

MS. COOPER: What happened then?

MS. CLEARY: The right book. It was *The Dutch Twins* by Lucy Fitch Perkins. I started to look at the pictures because I was bored, and I discovered that I was reading it and enjoying it!

MS. COOPER: That's a good feeling. And you were lucky to find a second book that you liked after that.

MS. CLEARY: Well, my mother had brought home *The Swiss Twins* and I read that the same day.

AWARD-WINNING AUTHOR

MS. COOPER: So she got you hooked on a series, like the Ramona books.

MS. CLEARY: Yes, my mother always kept books around the house, hoping that I would read, and she would read aloud to me. When I was in the fourth grade we moved near a branch library, which was heaven for me.

MS. COOPER: Did you write at all when you were that age?

MS. CLEARY: No.

MS. COOPER: You just did school writing?

MS. CLEARY: Just school assignments. But compositions were always my favorite assignments.

MS. COOPER: What advice would you give to young people who want to write?

MS. CLEARY: Writing doesn't have to be a story. Why not write a page of dialogue, such as a quarrel between a brother and sister? Be original and don't copy. Don't use characters from other people's books or television shows. Look around you and find your own characters. Good writing is original and comes from within the writer.

MS. COOPER: What do you think about keeping a diary or notebook?

MS. CLEARY: I think keeping a diary is useful.

MS. COOPER: How do you actually do your writing?

MS. CLEARY: Oh, I write with a pen in longhand. And then I type it up so I can see what it looks like.

MS. COOPER: What do you think is the hardest thing about writing, and what do you think is the easiest thing about writing?

MS. CLEARY: The hardest thing about writing is pushing through to the end of the story. The easiest thing is revising. I think all writers do some revising. That's when I cross out a lot and reduce a page to one paragraph. It's necessary because in my first draft I tend to put in extra material as it comes to mind. And then when I finish I realize that some of it wasn't needed.

MS. COOPER: Tell me more about pushing through to the end of the story. When you start a book, do you know how it's going to end?

MS. CLEARY: No I don't, and I don't always write stories in order. You have to wander in your imagination. In *Ramona and Her Father,* I wrote the last chapter first. It began as a short story, a Christmas story, I was asked to write for a magazine. And as I wrote it I began to think how the family got to this point. In a way I wrote that book backwards. I often begin in the middle. I begin with the characters and something they would do and just let the story work itself out.

MS. COOPER: That's interesting. You start in the middle and maybe one day you feel like writing about what happened before the incident, and then the next day . . .

137

MS. CLEARY: I write everything that's vivid to me. And it usually all fits together. Sometimes there's a chapter I have to leave out because it doesn't really belong in that book.

MS. COOPER: You might put it in another book?

MS. CLEARY: I might. Or I might tear it up. And also I have to enjoy what I'm writing. I've torn up two, well, fairly long manuscripts because I suddenly realized that they bored me. If it bores the author, it's going to bore the reader.

MS. COOPER: Some of the vivid incidents you're talking about—for example, Ramona breaking the egg over her head—did those things really happen, or did you just make them up?

MS. CLEARY: Well, both. I happened to hear about the egg incident when a group of teachers were talking. Sometimes I write about things that happened in my own childhood, but I change them. Sometimes I want to write about something, and it won't fit into the story. I wanted to write about the time my cat ate my jack-o'-lantern. And it took me about 20 years before that would work into a story.

MS. COOPER: So sometimes you just put an idea into the back of your mind and save it?

MS. CLEARY: Yes, I've had characters wandering about in the back of my mind who will not come into books.

MS. COOPER: They're just waiting for their own stories.

MS. CLEARY: Yes.

SCHOOL DAYS

What character traits do Beverly Cleary and Ramona Quimby have in common? Which of their character traits are different?

. . . .

Compare and contrast Ramona's opinion of *The Left-Behind Cat* to Ms. Cleary's opinion of *The Dutch Twins.*

. . . .

WRITER'S WORKSHOP Ramona starts to get excited about her book report when she is able to think of some good ideas for presenting it. Think about a time when you were excited about a school activity, such as a science experiment or a special project. Then write a personal narrative about it. Remember to include time-order words as you tell what happened at the beginning, in the middle, and at the end of your exciting event.

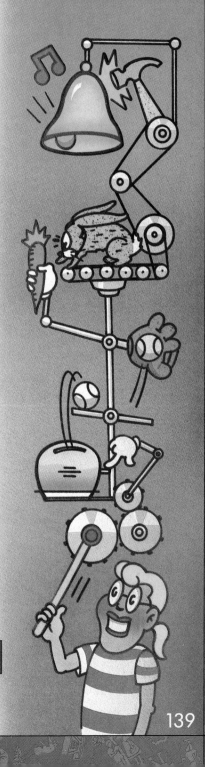

CARING AND SHARING

Giving a gift to someone shows that you care about that person. Giving of yourself not only shows you care but also is a very special way of sharing what you have with others. The following selections and poem tell about some special ways that children show they care.

CONTENTS

THROUGH GRANDPA'S EYES

by Patricia MacLachlan

illustrated by Greg Shed

Of all the houses that I know,
I like my grandpa's best. My friend
Peter has a new glass house with pebble-path
gardens that go nowhere. And Maggie lives next door
in an old wooden house with rooms behind rooms, all
with carved doors and brass doorknobs. They are fine
houses. But Grandpa's house is my favorite. Because I
see it through Grandpa's eyes.

Grandpa is blind. He doesn't see the house the way I do. He has his own way of seeing.

In the morning, the sun pushes through the curtains into my eyes. I burrow down into the covers to get away, but the light follows me. I give up, throw back the covers, and run to Grandpa's room.

The sun wakes Grandpa differently from the way it wakes me. He says it touches him, *warming* him awake. When I peek around the door, Grandpa is already up and doing his morning exercises. Bending and stretching by the bed. He stops and smiles because he hears me.

"Good morning, John."

"Where's Nana?" I ask him.

"Don't you know?" he says, bending and stretching. "Close your eyes, John, and look through my eyes."

I close my eyes. Down below, I hear the banging of pots and the sound of water running that I didn't hear before.

"Nana is in the kitchen, making breakfast," I say.

When I open my eyes again, I can see Grandpa nodding at me. He is tall with dark gray hair. And his eyes are sharp blue even though they are not sharp seeing.

I exercise with Grandpa. Up and down. Then I try to exercise with my eyes closed.

"One, two," says Grandpa, "three, four."

"Wait!" I cry. I am still on one, two when Grandpa is on three, four.

I fall sideways. Three times. Grandpa laughs as he hears my thumps on the carpet.

"Breakfast!" calls Nana from downstairs.

"I smell eggs frying," says Grandpa. He bends his head close to mine. "And buttered toast."

The wooden banister on the stairway has been worn smooth from Grandpa running his fingers up and down. I walk behind him, my fingers following Grandpa's smooth path.

We go into the kitchen.

"I smell flowers," says Grandpa.

"What flowers?" I ask.

He smiles. He loves guessing games.

"Not violets, John, not peonies . . ."

"Carnations!" I cry. *I* love guessing games.

"Silly." Grandpa laughs. "Marigolds. Right, Nana?"

Nana laughs, too.

"That's too easy," she says, putting two plates of food in front of us.

"It's not too easy," I protest. "How can Grandpa tell? All the smells mix together in the air."

"Close your eyes, John," says Nana. "Tell me what breakfast is."

"I smell the eggs. I smell the toast," I say, my eyes closed. "And something else. The something else doesn't smell good."

"*That* something else," says Nana smiling, "is the marigolds."

When he eats, Grandpa's plate of food is a clock.

"Two eggs at nine o'clock and toast at two o'clock," says Nana to Grandpa. "And a dollop of jam."

"A dollop of jam," I tell Grandpa, "at six o'clock."

I make my plate of food a clock, too, and eat through Grandpa's eyes.

After breakfast, I follow Grandpa's path through the dining room to the living room, to the window that he opens to feel the weather outside, to the table where he finds his pipe, and to his cello in the corner.

"Will you play with me, John?" he asks.

He tunes our cellos without looking. I play with a music stand and music before me. I know all about sharps and flats. I see them on the music. But Grandpa plays them. They are in his fingers. For a moment I close my eyes and play through Grandpa's eyes. My fingering hand slides up and down the cello neck—toward the pegs for flats, toward the bridge for sharps. But with my eyes closed my bow falls from the strings.

"Listen," says Grandpa. "I'll play a piece I learned when I was your age. It was my favorite."

He plays the tune while I listen. That is the way Grandpa learns new pieces. By listening.

"Now," says Grandpa. "Let's do it together."

"That's fine," says Grandpa as we play. "But C sharp, John," he calls to me. "C sharp!"

Later, Nana brings out her clay to sculpt my Grandpa's head.

"Sit still," she grumbles.

"I won't," he says, imitating her grumbly voice, making us laugh.

While she works, Grandpa takes out his piece of wood. He holds it when he's thinking. His fingers move back and forth across the wood, making smooth paths like the ones on the stair banister.

"Can I have a piece of thinking wood, too?" I ask.

Grandpa reaches in his shirt pocket and tosses a small bit of wood in my direction. I catch it. It is smooth with no splinters.

"The river is up," says Nana.

Grandpa nods a short nod. "It rained again last night. Did you hear the gurgling in the rain gutter?"

As they talk, my fingers begin a river on my thinking wood. The wood will winter in my pocket so when I am not at Grandpa's house I can still think about Nana, Grandpa, and the river.

When Nana is finished working, Grandpa runs his hand over the sculpture, his fingers soft and quick like butterflies.

"It looks like me," he says, surprised.

My eyes have already told me that it looks like Grandpa. But he shows me how to feel his face with my three middle fingers, and then the clay face.

"Pretend your fingers are water," he tells me.

My waterfall fingers flow down his clay head, filling in the spaces beneath the eyes like little pools before they flow down over the cheeks. It does feel like Grandpa. This time my fingers tell me.

Grandpa and I walk outside, through the front yard and across the field to the river. Grandpa has not been blind forever. He remembers in his mind the gleam of the sun on the river, the Queen Anne's lace in the meadow, and every dahlia in his garden. But he gently takes my elbow as we walk so that I can help show him the path.

"I feel a south wind," says Grandpa.

I can tell which way the wind is blowing because I see the way the tops of the trees lean. Grandpa tells by the feel of the meadow grasses and by the way his hair blows against his face.

When we come to the riverbank, I see that Nana was right. The water is high and has cut in by the willow tree. It flows around and among the roots of the tree, making paths. Paths like Grandpa's on the stair banister and on the thinking wood. I see a blackbird with a red patch on its wing sitting on a cattail. Without thinking, I point my finger.

"What is that bird, Grandpa?" I ask excitedly.

"Conk-a-ree," the bird calls to us.

"A red-winged blackbird," says Grandpa promptly.

He can't see my finger pointing. But he hears the song of the bird.

"And somewhere behind the blackbird," he says, listening, "a song sparrow."

I hear a scratchy song, and I look and look until I see the earth-colored bird that Grandpa knows is here.

Nana calls from the front porch of the house.

"Nana's made hot bread for lunch," he tells me happily. "And spice tea." Spice tea is his favorite.

I close my eyes, but all I can smell is the wet earth by the river.

As we walk back to the house, Grandpa stops suddenly. He bends his head to one side, listening. He points his finger upward.

"Honkers," he whispers.

I look up and see a flock of geese, high in the clouds, flying in a *V.*

"Canada geese," I tell him.

"Honkers," he insists. And we both laugh.

We walk up the path again and to the yard where Nana is painting the porch chairs. Grandpa smells the paint.

"What color, Nana?" he asks. "I cannot smell the color."

"Blue," I tell him, smiling. "Blue like the sky."

"Blue like the color of Grandpa's eyes," Nana says.

When he was younger, before I can remember, before he was blind, Grandpa did things the way I do. Now, when we drink tea and eat lunch on the porch, Grandpa pours his own cup of tea by putting his finger just inside the rim of the cup to tell him when it is full. He never burns his finger. Afterward, when I wash the dishes, he feels them as he dries them. He even sends some back for me to wash again.

"Next time," says Grandpa, pretending to be cross, "I wash, you dry."

In the afternoon, Grandpa, Nana, and I take our books outside to read under the apple tree. Grandpa reads his book with his fingers, feeling the raised Braille dots that tell him the words.

As he reads, Grandpa laughs out loud.

"Tell us what's funny," says Nana. "Read to us, Papa."

And he does.

Nana and I put down our books to listen. A gray squirrel comes down the trunk of the apple tree, tail high, and seems to listen, too. But Grandpa doesn't see him.

After supper, Grandpa turns on the television. I watch, but Grandpa listens, and the music and the words tell him when something is dangerous or funny, happy or sad.

Somehow, Grandpa knows when it is dark, and he takes me upstairs and tucks me into bed. He bends down to kiss me, his hands feeling my head.

"You need a haircut, John," he says.

Before Grandpa leaves, he pulls the light chain above my bed to turn out the light. But, by mistake, he's turned it on instead. I lie for a moment after he's gone, smiling, before I get up to turn off the light.

Then, when it is dark for me the way it is dark for Grandpa, I hear the night noises that Grandpa hears. The house creaking, the birds singing their last songs of the day, the wind rustling the tree outside my window.

Then, all of a sudden, I hear the sounds of geese overhead. They fly low over the house.

"Grandpa," I call softly, hoping he's heard them too.

"Honkers," he calls back.

"Go to sleep, John," says Nana.

Grandpa says her voice smiles to him. I test it.

"What?" I call to her.

"I said go to sleep," she answers.

She says it sternly. But Grandpa is right. Her voice smiles to me. I know. Because I'm looking through Grandpa's eyes.

THINK IT OVER

1. Name some of the ways John and Grandpa show their feelings for one another.

2. How does Grandpa read?

3. How are Grandpa's fingers like John's eyes?

4. What part of the story is most interesting to you? Tell why it is interesting.

WRITE

Write a description of an object for a friend. Use words that will help him or her "see" the object without actually looking at it.

Writers

by Jean Little
illustrated by Roberta Ludlow

Emily writes of poetic things
Like crocuses and hummingbirds' wings,
But I think people beat hummingbirds every time.

Emily likes to write of snow
And dawn and candlelight aglow,
But I'd rather write about me and Emily and stuff like that.

The funny thing is, I delight
To read what Emily likes to write,
And Emily says she thinks my poems are okay too.

Also, sometimes, we switch with each other.
Emily writes of a fight with her mother.
I tell about walking alone by the river,
  —how still and golden it was.

I know what Emily means, you see,
And, often, Emily's halfway me. . . .
Oh, there's just no way to make anybody else understand.

We're not a bit the same and yet,
We're closer than most people get.
There's no one word for it. We just care about each other
  the way we are supposed to.

So I can look through Emily's eyes
And she through mine. It's no surprise,
When you come right down to it, that we're friends.

AWARD-WINNING
AUTHOR

A Gift for Tía Rosa

by Karen T. Taha

"AROUND, OVER, THROUGH, AND PULL. Around, over, through, and pull," Carmela repeated as she knitted. A rainbow of red, orange, and gold wool stretched almost to her feet. Now and then she stopped and listened for her father's car. He mustn't see what she was knitting!

The rumble of a motor made her drop the needles and run to the window. In the gray November shadows, she saw a battered brown station wagon turn into the garage next door.

illustrated by Laura Kelly

"Mamá, she's home! Tía Rosa is home!" Carmela called. Carmela's mother hurried out of the bedroom. She put her arm around Carmela. They watched as lights flickered on in the windows, bringing the neat white house back to life.

"I know you want to see Tía Rosa, Carmela," said her mother, "but she and Tío Juan have had a long trip. Tía Rosa must be very tired after two weeks in the hospital."

"But can I call her, Mamá?" asked Carmela. "The scarf for Papá is almost done. She promised to help me fringe it when she came home."

"No, Carmela. Not now," her mother replied firmly. "Tía Rosa needs to rest." She smoothed back Carmela's thick black hair from her face.

Carmela tossed her head. "But Mamá . . . !"

"No, Carmela!"

Carmela knew there was no use arguing. But it wasn't fair. Tomorrow she would have to go to school. She couldn't see Tía Rosa until the afternoon. Her mother just didn't understand.

Frowning, Carmela plopped back on the sofa and picked up the silver knitting needles. At least she would finish more of the scarf before Tía Rosa saw it tomorrow. She bent over her knitting and began once more. "Around, over, through, and pull." The phone rang in the kitchen.

"I'll get it!" Carmela shouted, bounding into the hall. "Hello?" Her dark eyes sparkled. "Tía Rosa! You must see Papá's scarf. It's almost finished . . . You did? For me? Okay, I'll be right there!"

The phone clattered as Carmela hung up. "Mamá! Tía Rosa wants to see the scarf. She even brought me a surprise!"

Carmela's mother smiled and shook her head. "Tía Rosa is unbelievable."

Carmela stuffed the bright wool into her school bag. "I'm going to make Tía Rosa a surprise after I finish Papá's scarf!" she called as she ran out.

She ran across the yard to Tía Rosa's front door. The door swung open, and there was Tío Juan. He looked taller and thinner than she remembered, and his eyes looked sad.

Tío Juan was as tall as Tía Rosa was short, Carmela thought. He was as thin as Tía Rosa was plump. And he was as good at listening as Tía Rosa was at talking.

"*Hola*, Carmelita," he said, bending to kiss her cheek. He led her down the hall. "Tía Rosa is sitting up in bed. She's tired, but she wanted to see her favorite neighbor."

Tía Rosa in bed! In all her eight years Carmela had never seen Tía Rosa sick. She held her breath and peeked into the bedroom. Tía Rosa's round face crinkled into a smile when she saw Carmela.

"Carmelita, come give me a hug!"

Hugging Tía Rosa always made Carmela feel safe and warm. Tía Rosa was like a soft pillow that smelled of soap and bath powder and sometimes of sweet tamales. Now there was another smell, a dentist office smell, Carmela decided.

"Carmelita, I've missed you!" said Tía Rosa. "Let's look at what you have knitted."

Carmela handed her the scarf. Tía Rosa smiled. "Your papá will be proud to wear it," she said. "Tomorrow I'll show you how to fringe it, and I will start on the pink baby blanket for my granddaughter!"

Carmela laughed. "How do you know that Pepe's wife will have a girl?" she asked. Pepe was the oldest of Tía Rosa's six sons.

"Because," answered Tía Rosa with a grin, "anyone who has six sons and no daughters, deserves a granddaughter!"

"But Tía Rosa, what if the baby is a boy? Won't you love him just the same?"

"Of course," laughed Tía Rosa.

Carmela knew Tía Rosa would love the baby, boy or girl, but she crossed her fingers and wished for a girl, too.

"Now for the surprise!" said Tía Rosa. She handed Carmela a small white box. "Go on now. See what's inside."

Carmela opened the box carefully. A snowy ball of cotton lay inside. As she pulled at the cotton, her fingers touched something hard and very small. She heard the "clish" of a chain as she lifted the surprise from under the cotton. In her hand Carmela held a tiny silver rose on a fine chain.

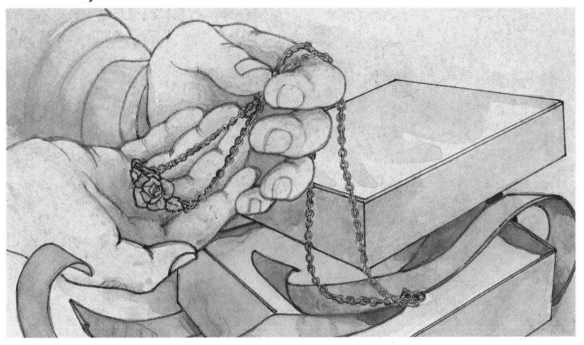

"Oh, Tía Rosa. It's beautiful!" exclaimed Carmela.

"The rose is so you'll remember your old Tía Rosa," she said.

"How could I forget you, Tía Rosa?" asked Carmela. "You're right here!"

Before she went home, Carmela put the rose around her neck. She promised to return the next day after school.

Carmela returned the next day, and the next, and every day for a whole week. Tía Rosa stayed in her room, and Tío Juan moved a chair by the bed for Carmela. Together the two friends worked on their surprise gifts.

"Why does Tía Rosa stay in bed all the time?" Carmela asked her father at breakfast one day.

Her father looked away for a moment. Then he took Carmela's hands in his. "Tía Rosa is very sick, Carmela. The doctors don't think she can get well," he explained.

"But Papá," said Carmela. "I have been sick lots of times. Remember when Tía Rosa stayed with me when you and Mamá had to go away?"

"Yes," answered her father. "But Tía Rosa . . ."

Carmela didn't listen. "Now I will stay with Tía Rosa until she gets well, too," she said.

Every afternoon Carmela worked on her father's scarf. The fringe was the easiest part. With Tía Rosa's help she would have the scarf finished long before Christmas.

Tía Rosa worked on the pink baby blanket, but the needles didn't fly in her sure brown fingers like they once did. Carmela teased her. "Tía Rosa, are you knitting slowly because you might have to change the pink yarn to blue when the baby is born?"

"No, no," replied Tía Rosa with a grin. "The baby will surely be a girl. We need girls in this family. You're the only one I have!"

Sometimes Tía Rosa fell asleep with her knitting still in her hands. Then Carmela would quietly put the needles and yarn into Tía Rosa's big green knitting bag and tiptoe out of the room.

Carmela liked Saturdays and Sundays best because she could spend more time at Tía Rosa's. Mamá always sent a plate of cookies with her, and Tío Juan made hot chocolate for them.

One Saturday morning when Carmela rang the doorbell, Tío Juan didn't come. Carmela ran to the garage and peeked in the window. The brown station wagon was gone.

She returned home and called Tía Rosa's number. The phone rang and rang. Carmela went down the steps to the basement. Her mother was rubbing stain into the freshly sanded wood of an old desk.

"Tía Rosa isn't home," said Carmela sadly. Her mother looked up from her work.

"I thought I heard a car in the night," said her mother. "Surely Tío Juan would have called us if . . ."

Just then the phone rang upstairs. Carmela heard footsteps creak across the floor as her father walked to answer it.

Moments later the footsteps thumped softly towards the basement door. Carmela's father came slowly down the steps. Carmela shivered when she saw his sad face. He put his arms around Carmela and her mother and hugged them close. "Tía Rosa is gone," he whispered. "She died early this morning."

No, her father's words couldn't be true. Carmela didn't believe it. Tía Rosa would come back. She had always come back before.

"It's not true!" cried Carmela. She broke away from her mother and father and raced up the stairs. She ran out the front door and through the yard to Tía Rosa's house. She pushed the doorbell again and again. She pounded on the silent door until her fists hurt. At last she sank down on the steps.

Later her father came. With a soft hanky he brushed the tears from her cheeks. At last they walked quietly home.

The next days were long and lonely for Carmela. She didn't care that Papá's finished scarf lay hidden in her closet, bright and beautiful. She didn't want to see it. She didn't want to feel the cool, smooth knitting needles in her hands ever again.

The white house next door was busy with people coming and going. Carmela took over food her mother and father cooked, but she quickly returned home. She didn't like to see Tío Juan. Seeing Tío Juan made her miss Tía Rosa even more.

One day Carmela said to her mother, "Tía Rosa died before I could give her anything, Mamá. She baked me cookies and taught me to knit and brought me surprises. I was going to surprise her. Now it's too late."

"Carmela, Tía Rosa didn't want her kindness returned. She wanted it passed on," said her mother. "That way a part of Tía Rosa will never die."

"But I wanted to give something to her!" shouted Carmela. "Just to Tía Rosa. To show her that I loved her!"

"She knew that, Carmela. Every smile and hug and visit told her that you loved her," said her mother. "Now it's Tío Juan who needs our love."

"I know," answered Carmela in a soft voice, "but it's hard, Mamá. It hurts so much without Tía Rosa."

One night Carmela's mother asked Tío Juan to dinner. Carmela met him at the door. This time Carmela did not turn away when she saw his sad eyes. Instead, she hugged him tightly.

For the first time in a week, Tío Juan smiled. "Carmelita, tomorrow you must come next door. I would like you to meet my new granddaughter. Her parents have named her Rosita, little Rose, after her grandmother."

Carmela looked down at her silver rose necklace so Tío Juan would not see the tears in her eyes. Tía Rosa knew the baby would be a girl. Then Carmela remembered the unfinished blanket. "Now I know what I can give!" she said.

After dinner Tío Juan went back to the white house. A few minutes later he returned with Tía Rosa's big knitting bag. Very carefully Carmela pulled out the half-finished blanket and wound the soft pink yarn around the needle.

"Around, over, through, and pull. Around, over, through, and pull." Carmela smiled. At last she had a gift for Tía Rosa.

THINK IT OVER

1. Name some of the ways Carmela and Tía Rosa showed that they cared for one another.

2. What gift did Carmela give for Tía Rosa?

3. Would you describe this story as a happy one or a sad one? Give reasons for your choice.

WRITE

What gave Carmela the idea for the perfect gift for Tía Rosa? Write a paragraph telling what made the gift perfect.

CARING AND SHARING

Think about John's grandpa and Tía Rosa. Which person do you think could live alone? Explain why you think as you do.

. . . .

Imagine that Carmela visits John's grandpa. What gift could she bring to him that he would enjoy?

. . . .

WRITER'S WORKSHOP   If you wanted to make a gift for a special person, what kind of gift would you make? Write directions someone might follow to make the gift. Your paragraph should tell what the gift is, the materials needed, and the steps to follow.

177

LEARNING ABOUT YOURSELF

Sometimes spending time with people you like gives you a chance to do new things. Perhaps it's because you learn from others. People often like to share what they know how to do or make with their friends. The story, the words from the author, and the recipe you are about to read may help you learn new things.

CONTENTS

SPENDING TIME WITH *Grandpa*

by Mildred Pitts Walter
illustrated by Brian Deines

Justin lives in the city and is usually surrounded by women—his mother and his two older sisters. Justin's sisters, Evelyn and Hadiya, often complain that he can't do anything right. He starts to believe he can't do "women's work," and the shame of it brings him to tears when his grandfather visits his family. When Justin stays on his grandpa's ranch for a while, he begins to look at things differently.

CORETTA SCOTT
KING AWARD

from *Justin and the Best Biscuits in the World*

GRANDPA'S HOUSE SAT about a mile in from the road.
Between that road and the house lay a large meadow with
a small stream. Everything seemed in order when Justin
and Grandpa arrived.

Justin got out and opened the gate to the winding road
that led toward the house. The meadow below shimmered
in waves of tall green grass. The horses grazed calmly
there. Justin was so excited to see them again that he
waved his grandpa on. "I'll walk up, Grandpa." He ran
down into the meadow.

Pink prairie roses blossomed near the fence. Goldenrod,
sweet William, and black-eyed Susans added color here
and there. Justin waded through the lush green grass.

The horses, drinking at the stream, paid no attention
as he raced across the meadow toward them. *Cropper looks
so old*, he thought as he came closer. But Black Lightning's
coat shone, as beautiful as ever. Justin gave a familiar
whistle. The horses lifted their heads and their ears went
back, but only Black moved toward him on the run.

Justin reached up and Black lowered his head. Justin rubbed him behind the ear. Softly he said, "Good boy, Black. I've missed you. You glad to see me?"

Then Pal nosed in, wanting to be petted, too.

Cropper didn't bother. Justin wondered if Cropper's eyesight was fading.

The sun had moved well toward the west. Long shadows from the rolling hills reached across the plains. "Want to take me home, boy?" Justin asked Black.

Black lowered his head and pawed with one foot as he shook his mane. Justin led him to a large rock. From the rock, Justin straddled Black's back, without a saddle. Black walked him home.

Grandpa's house stood on a hill surrounded by plains, near the rolling hills. Over many years, trees standing

close by the house had grown tall and strong. The house, more than a hundred years old, was made of logs. The sun and rain had turned the logs on the outside an iron gray. Flecks of green showed in some of the logs.

When Justin went inside, Grandpa had already changed his clothes. Now he busily measured food for the animals. While Grandpa was away, a neighbor had come to feed the pigs and chickens. The horses took care of themselves, eating and drinking in the meadow. Today the horses would have some oats, too.

"Let's feed the animals first," Grandpa said. "Then we'll cook the fish for dinner. You can clean them when we get back."

Justin sighed deeply. How could he tell Grandpa he didn't know how to clean fish? He was sure to make a mess of it. Worriedly, he helped Grandpa load the truck with the food and water for the chickens and pigs. They put in oats for the horses, too. Then they drove to the chicken yard.

As they rode along the dusty road, Justin remembered Grandpa telling him that long, long ago they had raised hundreds of cattle on Q-T Ranch. Then when Justin's mama was a little girl, they had raised only chickens on

the ranch, selling many eggs to people in the cities. Now Grandpa had only a few chickens, three pigs, and three horses.

At the chicken yard, chickens rushed around to get the bright yellow corn that Justin threw to them. They fell over each other, fluttering and clucking. While Justin fed them, Grandpa gathered the eggs.

The pigs lazily dozed in their pens. They had been wallowing in the mud pond nearby. Now cakes of dried mud dotted their bodies. The floor where they slept had mud on it, too. Many flies buzzed around. *My room surely doesn't look like this,* Justin thought.

The pigs ran to the trough when Grandpa came with the pail of grain mixed with water. They grunted and snorted. The smallest one squealed with delight. *He's cute,* Justin thought.

By the time they had fed the horses oats and returned home, it was dark and cooler. Justin was glad it was so late. Maybe now Grandpa would clean the fish so that they could eat sooner. He was hungry.

Grandpa had not changed the plan. He gave Justin some old newspapers, a small sharp knife, and a bowl with clean water.

"Now," he said, handing Justin the pail that held the fish, "you can clean these."

Justin looked at the slimy fish in the water. How could he tell his grandpa that he didn't want to touch those fish? He still didn't want Grandpa to know that he had never

cleaned fish before. Evelyn's words crowded him: *Can't do anything right.* He dropped his shoulders and sighed. "Do I have to, Grandpa?"

"We have to eat, don't we?"

"But—but I don't know how," Justin cried.

"Oh, it's not hard. I'll show you." Grandpa placed a fish on the newspaper. "Be careful now and keep it on this paper. When you're all done, just fold the paper and all the mess is inside."

Justin watched Grandpa scrape the fish upward from the tail toward the head. Little shiny scales came off easily. Then he cut the fish's belly upward from a little vent hole and scraped all the stuff inside onto the paper. "Now see how easy that is. You try," Grandpa said. "Be very careful with the knife." He watched Justin to see if he knew what to do.

Justin scraped the tiny scales off confidently. Then he hesitated. Screwing up his face, he shuddered as he cut, then pulled the insides out. Finally he got the knack of it.

Grandpa, satisfied that Justin would do fine, went into the kitchen to make a fire in the big stove.

Later that evening, Justin felt proud when Grandpa let him put the fish on the table.

After dinner, they sat in the living room near the huge fireplace. Great-Great-Grandma Ward had used that same fireplace to cook her family's meals.

Justin looked at the fireplace, trying to imagine how it must have been then. *How did people cook without a stove?* He knew Grandpa's stove was nothing like his mama's. Once that big iron stove got hot there was no way to turn it off or to low or to simmer. You just set the pots in a cooler place on the back of Grandpa's stove.

"Grandpa, how did your grandma cook bread in this fireplace?" he asked.

"Cooking bread in this fireplace was easy for my grandma. She once had to bake her bread on a hoe."

"But a hoe is for making a garden, Grandpa."

"Yes, I know, and it was that kind of hoe that she used. She chopped cotton with her hoe down in Tennessee. There was no fireplace in the family's little one-room house, so she cooked with a fire outside. She had no nice iron pots and skillets like I have now in the kitchen.

"At night when the family came in from the cotton

fields, Grandma made a simple bread with cornmeal and a little flour. She patted it and dusted it with more flour. Then she put it on the iron hoe and stuck it in the ashes. When it was nice and brown the ashes brushed off easily."

"How did they ever get from Tennessee to Missouri?"

"Justin, I've told you that so many times."

"I know, Grandpa. But I like to hear it. Tell me again."

"As a boy, my grandpa was a slave. Right after slavery my grandpa worked on a ranch in Tennessee. He rode wild mustangs and tamed them to become good riding horses. He cared so much about horses, he became a cowboy.

"He got married and had a family. Still he left home for many weeks, sometimes months, driving thousands of cattle over long trails. Then he heard about the government giving away land in the West through the Homestead Act. You only had to build a house and live in it to keep the land."

"So my great-great-grandpa built this house." Justin stretched out on the floor. He looked around at the walls that were now dark brown from many years of smoke from the fireplace.

"Just the room we're in now," Grandpa said.

"I guess every generation of Wards has added something. Now, my daddy, Phillip, added on the kitchen and the room right next to this one that is the dining room.

"I built the bathroom and the rooms upstairs. Once we had a high loft. I guess you'd call it an attic. I made that into those rooms upstairs. So you see, over the years this house has grown and grown. Maybe when you're a man, you'll bring your family here," Grandpa said.

"I don't know. Maybe. But I'd have to have an electric kitchen."

"As I had to have a bathroom with a shower. Guess that's progress," Grandpa said, and laughed.

"Go on, Grandpa. Tell me what it was like when Great-Great-Grandpa first came to Missouri."

"I think it's time for us to go to bed."

"It's not that late," Justin protested.

"For me it is. We'll have to get up early. I'll have to ride fence tomorrow. You know, in winter Q-T Ranch becomes a feeder ranch for other people's cattle. In spring, summer, and early fall cattle roam and graze in the high country. In winter when the heavy frosts come and it's bitter cold, they return to the plains. Many of those cattle feed at Q-T.

I have to have my fences mended before fall so the cattle can't get out."

"Can I ride fence with you?" Justin asked.

"Sure you can. Maybe you'll like riding fence. That's a man's work." Grandpa laughed.

Justin remembered that conversation in his room about women's work, and the tears. He burned with shame. He didn't laugh.

Upstairs, Grandpa gave Justin sheets and a blanket for his bed. "It'll be cool before morning," he told Justin. "You'll need this blanket. Can you make your bed?"

Justin frowned. He hated making his bed. But he looked at Grandpa and said, "I'm no baby." Justin joined Grandpa in laughter.

Grandpa went to his room. When he was all ready for bed, he came and found Justin still struggling to make his bed. Those sheets had to be made nice and smooth to impress Grandpa, Justin thought, but it wasn't easy.

Grandpa watched. "Want to see how a man makes a bed?" Grandpa asked.

Justin didn't answer. Grandpa waited. Finally, Justin, giving up, said, "Well, all right."

"Let's do it together," Grandpa said. "You on the other side."

Grandpa helped him smooth the bottom sheet and tuck it under the mattress at the head and foot of the bed. Then he put on the top sheet and blanket and smoothed them carefully.

"Now, let's tuck those under the mattress only at the foot of the bed," he said.

"That's really neat, Grandpa," Justin said, impressed.

"That's not it, yet. We want it to stay neat, don't we? Now watch." Grandpa carefully folded the covers in equal triangles and tucked them so that they made a neat corner at the end of the mattress. "Now do your side exactly the way I did mine."

Soon Justin was in bed. When Grandpa tucked him in, he asked, "How does it feel?"

Justin flexed his toes and ankles. "Nice. Snug."

"Like a bug in a rug?"

Justin laughed. Then Grandpa said, "That's how a man makes a bed."

Still laughing, Justin asked, "Who taught *you* how to make a bed? Your grandpa?"

"No. My grandma." Grandpa grinned and winked at Justin. "Good night."

Justin lay listening to the winds whispering in the trees. Out of his window in the darkness he saw lightning bugs flashing, heard crickets chirping. But before the first hoot of an owl, he was fast asleep.

THE SUN BEAMED down and sweat rolled off Justin as he rode on with Grandpa, looking for broken wires in the fence. They were well away from the house, on the far side of the ranch. Flies buzzed around the horses and now gnats swarmed in clouds just above their heads. The prairie resounded with songs of the bluebirds, the bobwhite quails, and the mockingbirds mimicking them all. The cardinal's song, as lovely as any, included a whistle.

It was well past noon and Justin was hungry. Soon they came upon a small, well-built shed, securely locked. Nearby was a small stream. Grandpa reined in his horse. When he and Justin dismounted, they hitched the horses, and unsaddled them.

"We'll have our lunch here," Grandpa said. Justin was surprised when Grandpa took black iron pots, other cooking utensils, and a table from the shed. Justin helped him remove some iron rods that Grandpa carefully placed over a shallow pit. These would hold the pots. Now Justin understood why Grandpa had brought uncooked food. They were going to cook outside.

First they collected twigs and cow dung. Grandpa called it cowchips. "These," Grandpa said, holding up a dried brown pad, "make the best fuel. Gather them up."

There were plenty of chips left from the cattle that had fed there in winter. Soon they had a hot fire.

Justin watched as Grandpa carefully washed his hands and then began to cook their lunch.

"When I was a boy about your age, I used to go with my father on short runs with cattle. We'd bring them down from the high country onto the plains."

"Did you stay out all night?"

"Sometimes. And that was the time I liked most. The cook often made for supper what I am going to make for lunch."

Grandpa put raisins into a pot with a little water and placed them over the fire. Justin was surprised when Grandpa put flour in a separate pan. He used his fist to make a hole right in the middle of the flour. In that hole he placed some shortening. Then he added water. With his long delicate fingers he mixed the flour, water, and shortening until he had a nice round mound of dough.

Soon smooth circles of biscuits sat in an iron skillet with a lid on top. Grandpa put the skillet on the fire with some of the red-hot chips scattered over the lid.

Justin was amazed. How could only those ingredients make good bread? But he said nothing as Grandpa put the chunks of smoked pork in a skillet and started them cooking. Soon the smell was so delicious, Justin could hardly wait.

Finally Grandpa suggested that Justin take the horses to drink at the stream. "Keep your eyes open and don't step on any snakes."

Justin knew that diamondback rattlers sometimes lurked around. They were dangerous. He must be careful. He watered Black first.

While watering Pal, he heard rustling in the grass. His heart pounded. He heard the noise again. He wanted to run, but was too afraid. He looked around carefully. There were two black eyes staring at him. He tried to pull Pal away from the water, but Pal refused to stop drinking. Then Justin saw the animal. It had a long tail like a rat's.

But it was as big as a cat. Then he saw something crawling on its back. They were little babies, hanging on as the animal ran.

A mama opossum and her babies, he thought, and was no longer afraid.

By the time the horses were watered, lunch was ready. "*M-mm-m,*" Justin said as he reached for a plate. The biscuits were golden brown, yet fluffy inside. And the sizzling pork was now crisp. Never had he eaten stewed raisins before.

"Grandpa, I didn't know you could cook like this," Justin said when he had tasted the food. "I didn't know men could cook so good."

"Why, Justin, some of the best cooks in the world are men."

The look he gave Grandpa revealed his doubts.

"It's true," Grandpa said. "All the cooks on the cattle trail were men. In hotels and restaurants they call them chefs."

"How did you make these biscuits?"

"That's a secret. One day I'll let you make some."

"Were you a cowboy, Grandpa?"

"I'm still a cowboy."

"No, you're not."

"Yes, I am. I work with cattle, so I'm a cowboy."

"You know what I mean. The kind who rides bulls, broncobusters. That kind of cowboy."

"No, I'm not that kind. But I know some."

"Are they famous?"

"No, but I did meet a real famous Black cowboy once. When I was eight years old, my grandpa took me to meet his friend Bill Pickett. Bill Pickett was an old man then. He had a ranch in Oklahoma."

"Were there lots of Black cowboys?"

"Yes. Lots of them. They were hard workers, too. They busted broncos, branded calves, and drove cattle.

My grandpa tamed wild mustangs."

"Bet they were famous."

"Oh, no. Some were. Bill Pickett created the sport of bulldogging. You'll see that at the rodeo. One cowboy named Williams taught Rough Rider Teddy Roosevelt how to break horses; and another one named Clay taught Will Rogers, the comedian, the art of roping." Grandpa offered Justin the last biscuit.

When they had finished their lunch they led the horses away from the shed to graze. As they watched the horses, Grandpa went on, "Now, there were some more very famous Black cowboys. Jessie Stahl. They say he was the best rider of wild horses in the West."

"How could he be? Nobody ever heard about him. I didn't."

Jessie Stahl

"Oh, there're lots of famous Blacks you never hear or read about. You ever hear about Deadwood Dick?"

Justin laughed. "No."

"There's another one. His real name was Nate Love.

Nate Love

He could outride, outshoot anyone. In Deadwood City in the Dakota Territory, he roped, tied, saddled, mounted, and rode a wild horse faster than anyone. Then in the shooting match, he hit the bull's-eye every time. The people named him Deadwood Dick right on the spot. Enough about cowboys, now. While the horses graze, let's clean up here and get back to our men's work."

Justin felt that Grandpa was still teasing him, the way he had in Justin's room when he had placed his hand on Justin's shoulder. There was still the sense of shame whenever the outburst about women's work and the tears were remembered.

As they cleaned the utensils and dishes, Justin asked, "Grandpa, you think housework is women's work?"

"Do you?" Grandpa asked quickly.

"I asked you first, Grandpa."

"I guess asking you that before I answer is unfair. No, I don't. Do you?"

"Well, it seems easier for them," Justin said as he splashed water all over, glad he was outside.

"Easier than for me?"

"Well, not for you, I guess, but for me, yeah."

"Could it be because you don't know how?"

"You mean like making the bed and folding the clothes."

"Yes." Grandpa stopped and looked at Justin. "Making the bed is easy now, isn't it? All work is that way. It doesn't matter who does the work, man or woman, when it needs to be done. What matters is that we try to learn how to do it the best we can in the most enjoyable way."

"I don't think I'll ever like housework," Justin said, drying a big iron pot.

"It's like any other kind of work. The better you do it, the easier it becomes, and we seem not to mind doing things that are easy."

With the cooking rods and all the utensils put away, they locked the shed and went for their horses.

"Now, I'm going to let you do the cinches again. You'll like that."

There's that teasing again, Justin thought. "Yeah. That's a man's work," he said, and mounted Black.

"There are some good horsewomen. You'll see them at the rodeo."

Grandpa mounted Pal. They went on their way, riding along silently, scanning the fence.

Finally Justin said, "I was just kidding, Grandpa." Then without planning to, he said, "I bet you don't like boys who cry like babies."

"Do I know any boys who cry like babies?"

"Aw, Grandpa, you saw me crying."

"Oh, I didn't think you were crying like a baby. In your room, you mean? We all cry sometime."

"You? Cry, Grandpa?"

"Sure."

They rode on, with Grandpa marking his map. Justin remained quiet, wondering what could make a man like Grandpa cry.

As if knowing Justin's thoughts, Grandpa said, "I remember crying when you were born."

"Why? Didn't you want me?"

"Oh, yes. You were the most beautiful baby. But, you see, your grandma, Beth, had just died. When I held you I was flooded with joy. Then I thought, *Grandma will never see this beautiful boy.* I cried."

The horses wading through the grass made the only sound in the silence. Then Grandpa said, "There's an old saying, son. 'The brave hide their fears, but share their tears.' Tears bathe the soul."

Justin looked at his grandpa. Their eyes caught. A warmth spread over Justin and he lowered his eyes. He wished he could tell his grandpa all he felt, how much he loved him.

THINK IT OVER

1. Do you think Justin felt good about himself at the end of the story? Tell why you think as you do.

2. Do you think a person can learn to do something by listening to someone explain how to do it? Explain why.

3. What foods do you know how to prepare that you could teach Justin to make?

WRITE

Think about what Justin learned while he stayed with his grandfather. Pretend you are Justin and write a letter to your mother telling her what you learned.

WORDS
about the
Author:
Mildred Pitts Walter

Mildred Pitts Walter was born in Louisiana, the youngest of seven children. Her father was a log cutter, and the family lived in two small houses owned by the lumber company. They used one house for sleeping and the other for daytime activities such as cooking and washing. The yards of the two houses were used as a community meeting place. On Saturday nights, the neighbors gathered there for food, games, singing, storytelling, and dancing.

Young Mildred was eager for school to start each fall so she could read the school's library books. She spent the summers of her school years working to earn money for college. She was graduated from Southern University in Scotlandville, Louisiana.

After graduation, Mildred taught kindergarten and elementary grades. She also helped organize a program called Head Start. This program prepares

young children for school so that they will do well once they start.

Ms. Walter wanted better books for the students in her classes. Someone suggested that she write the books herself, so she did!

Mildred Walter writes about what she knows well—family life, problems at school, and the struggles of black people. Her years spent as a teacher help her write about the characters in her stories. She tries to understand her characters just as she tried to understand her students. She feels that an author needs to notice details that other people may miss.

As a child, Mildred was allowed to make choices, and learned to live with the results. Now she uses this idea in her stories. The characters in her books often face difficult choices, as Justin did in "Spending Time with Grandpa." When her characters use courage to make a choice, they are able to make changes in their lives.

WHAT'S GORP?

GORP IS GOOD OLD RAISINS AND PEANUTS!

MAKE YOUR OWN

GORP

This is how to prepare a quick and easy snack for yourself and a friend. Measure these ingredients into a plastic bag:

½ cup raisins
½ cup unsalted peanuts
½ cup sunflower seeds
½ cup chopped dates

Be sure the bag is tightly closed, then shake it. Your snack is ready to share with a friend and enjoy.

ILLUSTRATED BY JACKIE SNIDER

206

LEARNING ABOUT YOURSELF

Do you think that Justin will want to visit his grandfather's ranch again? Explain why you think as you do.

. . . .

Think about the recipe you read for making GORP. Do you think it is easy for Justin's grandfather to remember the recipe for making biscuits? Explain your answer.

. . . .

WRITER'S WORKSHOP Imagine that you were a cowhand during the time of Bill Pickett, Jessie Stahl, Nate Love, or other Black cowboys. What was life like then? To find out, write a short biography about one of those cowboys. Be sure to include details such as the dates of birth and death, where he lived and worked, and why he is remembered. You may want to use an encyclopedia or books about cowboys to research the facts for your report.

CONNECTIONS

Antonia Novello

MULTICULTURAL CONNECTION

FRIENDS ARE PEOPLE WHO CARE

When Antonia Novello was a child in Puerto Rico, she had a health problem. Every summer she spent time in the hospital. She came to think of her kind doctors as friends.

Antonia decided to be a doctor herself. Her parents encouraged her through years of hard study. She became a doctor and began running health care programs that helped millions of people.

Today Dr. Novello is the surgeon general of the United States and is in charge of our nation's public health program. She especially wants to help children. Like the childhood doctors who were her models, she cares for others through her work.

■ Write a paragraph about a person who helps others. Publish your work in a class book titled "A Friend Is Someone Who Cares."

SOCIAL STUDIES CONNECTION

SPECIAL PEOPLE—SPECIAL PLACES

Antonia Novello came from Puerto Rico. With
your classmates, find out some interesting facts
about this island. Use the facts to make a collage
of pictures and words that tells about this special
place.

A drawing like this web can help you sort the
facts you find.

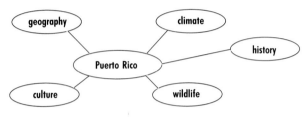

HEALTH CONNECTION

STAYING HEALTHY

Think about how Antonia Novello helped
people stay healthy. Then make a poster that
shows some good health tips. Share your poster
with your classmates.

UNIT ADVENTURES THREE

Adventure and mystery may be as far away as a bear from Peru or a trip to a lake. They may also be as near as a picture you paint. As you read the selections in this unit, look for the different ways the authors and illustrators share adventure. What does Allen Say tell about an Asian American family's camping adventure? How does Paul Sierra, a painter from Chicago who grew up in Cuba, use paint to create mystery? The selections in this unit will give you a chance to find out.

PICTURE THIS!

MYSTERIES TO SOLVE

GONE CAMPING

BOOKSHELF

VINEGAR PANCAKES AND VANISHING CREAM
by Bonnie Pryor

Martin Elwood Snodgrass sometimes feels as though everybody in his family is special in some way except him. A camping trip gives him the chance to look at himself and members of his family differently.

AWARD-WINNING AUTHOR

HBJ LIBRARY BOOK

PICNIC WITH PIGGINS
by Jane Yolen

The picnic with Piggins has been delightful until . . . CRASH! SPLASH! Rexy, one of the Reynard kits, disappears, leaving baffling clues. Only Piggins can decode the curious note and unravel the mystery.

AWARD-WINNING AUTHOR

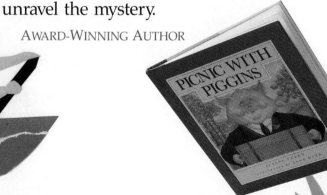

A RIVER DREAM

written and illustrated by Allen Say

A young boy who is sick receives a gift from his uncle. When he opens the gift box, a fantastic adventure begins. NEW YORK TIMES BEST ILLUSTRATED BOOKS OF THE YEAR

HUGH PINE & THE GOOD PLACE

by Janwillem van de Wetering

Hugh Pine is a very clever porcupine who is great at solving everybody's problems except his own. Hugh thinks things will be different when he finds the perfect place to live.

ALL I SEE

by Cynthia Rylant

This unusual story tells of the friendship between a child who paints and an artist. Pictures aren't the only things that appear on the canvas. CHILDREN'S CHOICE

PICTURE THIS!

Each day you face adventures, although you usually don't think about them. The adventures can be happy or sad. They can be adventures that you experience alone or with others. The unusual adventures in the selections and poem that follow should make you smile and laugh.

C O N T E N T S

What
the Mailman
Brought

Carolyn Craven   Tomie dePaola

Sunday morning it was raining. William Beauregard had missed the first week of school in his new city, and he was about to miss the second. William was sick. He had started feeling better now, but the doctor had been firm. "You need a lot of rest, my friend," he had said yesterday. "Another week at home, and no running up and down stairs."

William had nothing to do. He had read all his books twice. His train was broken. And he had eaten all the snacks he could eat.

William stared out the window. His old street had front porches, and big lawns, and lots of friends to play with. But William didn't know a single person in the new city. He walked around the room, and then he sat down at his desk. On his largest piece of paper he wrote in big black letters

SICK

He thought a moment. Then he added

OF
THIS

He took his sign to the window and taped it
there, so the writing faced out. Maybe someone
would see it. Afterward, William climbed in bed
and pulled the blankets over his head.

The next morning when William woke up he was
surprised to find a big flat parcel on his desk. He
ripped off the brown paper and took out three
paintbrushes and a palette. Under these was a pad
of thick white pebbly paper. And then he found
twelve tubes of paint in their own wooden box.

"Real paints!" William whispered. Mr. and Mrs. Beauregard were pleased too.

"I found the package on the doorstep last night," said his mother. "Who do you suppose it's from? I didn't think anyone knew you were sick."

His father brought a jar of water, and then his parents left him to paint.

William sat down at his desk and looked out the window. He saw a row of black iron railings. He saw white lace curtains. He saw grey chimneys. It was Monday morning, and no one was on the street.

Suddenly a figure came around the corner. It was the mailman. Or it looked like the mailman, wearing a blue uniform and pushing a little brown cart. But there was something funny about him. William shut his eyes for a minute, but when he opened them, the mailman looked just as strange. In fact, William thought, he looked very much like a . . .

All at once William remembered his paints. He squeezed out blobs onto the palette and dipped his brush. And he began to paint as the mailman waddled from mailbox to mailbox.

It was late afternoon when his father came upstairs.

"Will, what a great picture," his father said. "Where did you get the idea for it?"

Just then his mother came home from work and ran upstairs too.

"William, another package has come for you. It's marked FRAGILE in big red letters."

William opened the cardboard box and dug through crumpled tissue paper. Under it all was an enormous pale blue egg, smooth and hard and faintly speckled. All three Beauregards gasped.

"What kind of egg could it be?"

"Who could have sent it?"

William said nothing. He was thinking hard. He looked over at his picture. He looked at his egg.

"I think the mailman laid it," he said.

"The mailman *what?*"

"The mailman left it," William said quickly.

"Of course, Will," his father said. "But . . ."

Mrs. Beauregard got up and stroked his head. "I'll bring up your dinner, dear, since the doctor said no stairs."

The next day at eleven, William sat down at his desk. It was still raining, and the street was greyer than ever.

Then something caught his eye.

It was the mailman. Or was it? His nose was long and green and scaly, and he seemed to have a lot of pointed teeth. William was glad he was on the third floor. He painted fast and finished just as the mailman turned the corner and disappeared. He taped the painting up and crawled into bed.

Just before dinnertime, Mrs. Beauregard came up to his room with a box.

"William, another one!" she said.

William pulled it open and took out a shirt. It was covered with purple palm trees. "See Sunny Florida," William read from large letters across the back.

"Nana's the only person we know in Florida,"
murmured his mother. "But she hates purple."

William thought. Then he looked up.

"Do alligators live in Florida?"

"Yes, in the swamps. Why do you ask?"

But William didn't say anything, and soon his
mother went downstairs.

Even before William had opened his eyes on
Wednesday morning, he knew it was still raining. But
when he put on his new shirt, he felt more cheerful.
He ate the breakfast his father brought up and
squeezed new paint onto his palette.

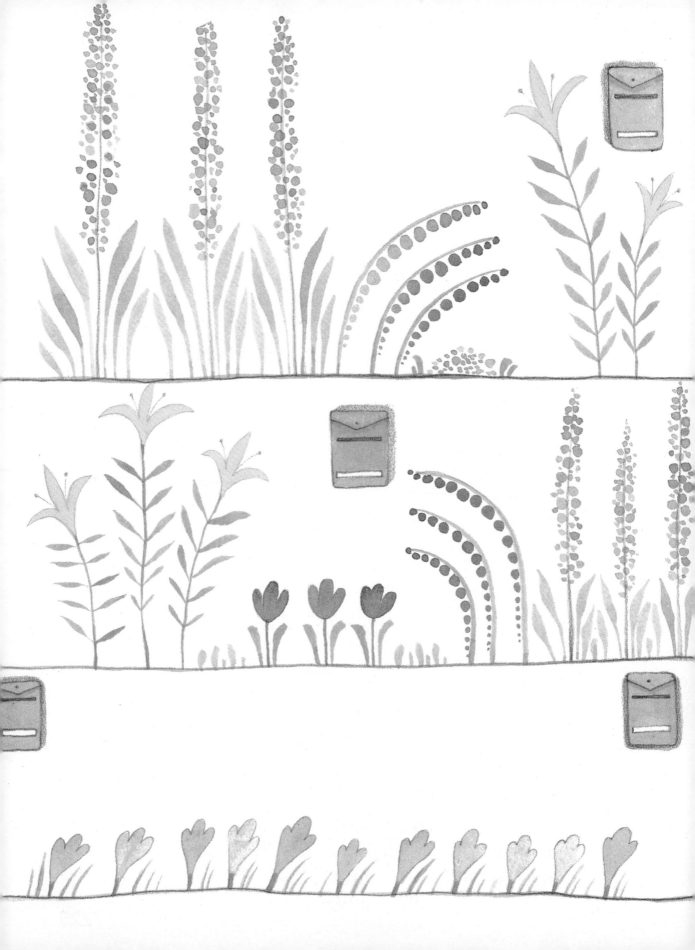

The mailman came around the corner waving a long and furry tail. It was striped black and white. William made sure his window was closed tight. Then he started to paint.

When Mr. and Mrs. Beauregard came upstairs that evening with the next package, he was reading in bed.

"William, it's not fair," his father said. "You get all the surprises."

"I'm a little worried about what *he's* left me," said William as he slowly untied the string.

"What *who's* left you?"

William didn't answer.

"Flowers!" his mother cried. "But where are
they from?"

William sniffed. "Mmmmm. Do you like my
painting?" he asked her.

She untaped it from the window. "Well, it's very
nice. Let's go find a vase," she said to his father.

Out in the hall she lowered her voice. "Wallace,
I'm a little worried about William. He paints such
strange pictures and he won't answer my questions
anymore."

"I'll have a talk with him tomorrow," his father said.

Mr. Beauregard went up to see William just before eleven the next day. The two of them looked out at the wet street.

"Well, Will, what are you painting today?"

"The mailman," William said.

His father stood up and walked around the room. "Will, do these animals in your pictures ever frighten you?"

William saw the mailman slide around the corner. "Of course not. They're very friendly."

His father patted his shoulder. "Don't tire yourself out," he said, and went down to his study.

Under the mailman's cap, William saw a shiny silver face. It had round eyes that didn't blink. William took his time painting. "This one is the best," he thought.

William's mother came upstairs at dinner-time carrying an omelette and a heavy box. They opened it together. William lifted out a spiky, spiraled shell. It was a deep rose color, fading to the most delicate pink.

William held it to his ear and heard a roar like the ocean. "It's a conch," his mother said, and stared at it thoughtfully. "I just don't understand," she finally said as she left.

Friday morning William laughed when a fat and furry mailman came into sight. William began to paint as the mailman slowly wriggled himself through the drizzle to the mailboxes. The picture was even better than the last one.

That evening both his parents came upstairs and sat on his bed. There was no box.

"Your doctor's appointment is at ten forty-five, Will," his father said. "Maybe he'll have good news." He reached in his pocket. "Your mother almost missed this one. It had rolled off the front step."

Mr. Beauregard handed him what looked like a
plain cotton ball. All three of them stared at it lying
in William's palm.

Suddenly William jumped.

"It moved!" he cried.

"Be careful!" his mother said.

As they watched, the cotton ball began to crack
down the middle. Something inside was pushing it
apart. It seemed to take forever.

"It's a cocoon, and it's hatching," whispered Mr.
Beauregard. Presently the butterfly pulled its way
out and clung to William's finger. They watched
the wings take color as the butterfly slowly waved
them dry.

"Let her crawl onto a pencil so you can go to bed,
Will," his father said.

Settled in his bed, William wondered what would arrive tomorrow. Suddenly he remembered tomorrow was Saturday, and he had a doctor's appointment. He would miss the mailman, he thought sadly.

"We're having a picnic!" said William's mother on their way home from the doctor's the next day. When they arrived, Mr. Beauregard was already spreading a blanket on the little terrace. The air smelled fresh and wet, and sunshine had begun to dry the puddles.

"What's the news, William?" his father asked.

"School on Monday," he answered. "I'm all better. Let's eat!"

William was halfway through his chocolate when he remembered.

"Did the mailman come?" he asked.

"Yes—as a matter of fact we had a chat. He's been out sick all week, just like you. And sorry, Will, he didn't bring any packages."

"The other ones came later in the day, though," said Mrs. Beauregard.

"I don't think there will be one today," William said. "Yesterday was the last."

They looked at him.

"How do you know, Will?" asked Mr. Beauregard.

"Just a feeling," said William. He was watching a big red butterfly float over their heads toward the south. William waved at the fluttery wings. "Can I wear my purple shirt to school on Monday?"

THINK IT OVER

1. Do you think the packages the mail carriers brought made William feel better? Why do you think as you do?

2. Name the animals that delivered packages to William. Then tell what was in each package William received.

3. How did William know that he wouldn't be getting a package on Saturday?

4. If you were William, which gift would you have enjoyed the most? Explain why.

WRITE

Think about the events that happened during the second week that William was sick. Imagine that he was sick for a third week. Write a paragraph about an adventure he might have had on one of his sick days.

The Secret Place

**written and illustrated
by Tomie dePaola**

It was my secret place—
   down at the foot
   of my bed—
   under the covers.

It was very white.

I went there
   with a book, a flashlight,
   and the special pencil
   that my grandfather gave me.

To read—
   and to draw pictures
   on all that white.

It was my secret place
   for about a week—

Until my mother came
   to change the sheets.

239

AWARD-WINNING
AUTHOR

240

PADDINGTON PAINTS A PICTURE

from PADDINGTON ON STAGE
adapted by Alfred Bradley and Michael Bond • illustrated by Peggy Fortnum

CAST OF CHARACTERS

MR. BROWN

PADDINGTON

MR. GRUBER

MRS. BIRD

MISS BLACK

MRS. BROWN

JONATHAN

JUDY

MAN

PROPS

In the Browns'
sitting room:
    A few chairs
    Table
    Easel
For scene II:
    suitcase

In Mr. Gruber's shop:
    Chair
    Sign saying "Antiques"
    Thermos flask, two mugs and a bun
    Pile of bric-a-brac, china, books, toys
    ★Half-restored "painting"

In the sitting room, for scenes III and IV:
    Very messy painting
    Paintbrush
    Paints—red and green
    Marmalade jar
    Spoon
    Palette (can be made from cardboard)
    Three empty bottles, painted to look as if they
    contain paint remover, ketchup and mustard
    Handkerchief
    Washing-up liquid
    Slip of paper for cheque

241

In this play the easel with Mr. Brown's painting should be placed near the centre of the stage so that Paddington has plenty of room to work on it. We don't need to see the painting, as it will be facing away from us until Miss Black brings it back at the end of the play. Of course, the tomato ketchup and mustard and paint remover should not be real (use empty bottles painted to look full), and the painting should be done beforehand so that it is dry for the performance. The painting should look as messy as you can make it.

When we get to Mr. Gruber's shop, all that we need to see is a pile of oddments with a notice saying "Antiques." Mr. Gruber should have a chair to sit on, a half-cleaned picture with a boat on one side and part of a lady's face on the other★, a Thermos flask and two mugs.

Scene One

[*The Browns' sitting room.* MR. BROWN *is getting ready to go to work as* PADDINGTON *comes in. The easel is standing with its back to the audience.*]

MR. BROWN   Hello, Paddington. What are your plans for today?

PADDINGTON   I think I might do some shopping, Mr. Brown. I like shopping.

MR. BROWN   You won't get lost?

PADDINGTON   No, I won't be going very far. Is your painting finished, Mr. Brown?

MR. BROWN   Yes. [*He looks at it.*] You know, I really think it's the best I've ever done.

PADDINGTON   I hope you win a prize.

MR. BROWN   Oh, I don't expect I shall. But it's fun. That's the important thing, I suppose. I must be off now. I'm late for work already. [*He goes to the door.*] Goodbye, Paddington. I'll see you tonight.

PADDINGTON   Goodbye, Mr. Brown.

[MR. BROWN *goes, and* PADDINGTON *takes a closer look at the painting.*]

I think I would enjoy painting. It looks *very* interesting.

Scene Two

[*Mr. Gruber's bric-a-brac shop in the Portobello Road. He is cleaning an oil painting when* PADDINGTON *arrives.*]

MR. GRUBER   Good morning. Can I help you?

PADDINGTON   [*putting down his suitcase*] I don't know really. I was out for a walk and your shop looked so nice, I thought I would like to see inside.

MR. GRUBER   Please have a look round, Mr. . . . er . . .

PADDINGTON   Brown. Paddington Brown. I come from Darkest Peru.

MR. GRUBER   Darkest Peru? How strange. I know Peru quite well. I spent a lot of my early life in South America.

PADDINGTON   Fancy that, Mr. . . . er . . .

MR. GRUBER   Gruber. Look . . . I've just made some cocoa, Mr. Brown. Would you care for a cup?

PADDINGTON   Ooh, yes, please.

MR. GRUBER   It's quite hot. I keep it in a vacuum.

PADDINGTON   [*amazed*] You keep your cocoa in a vacuum cleaner?

MR. GRUBER   No, Mr. Brown, a vacuum flask. [*He pours some cocoa and hands it to* PADDINGTON.] There's nothing like a chat over a bun and a cup of cocoa.

PADDINGTON   A bun as well! [*They sit down to enjoy their elevenses.*[1]] What were you doing when I came into the shop, Mr. Gruber?

MR. GRUBER   I was cleaning a painting. [*He picks it up.*] Now, what do you think of that?

---

[1]elevenses: a snack taken in the middle of the morning

PADDINGTON   [*looking at it*] It's a puzzle, Mr. Gruber. One half is a boat and the other half is a lady in a large hat.

MR. GRUBER   There you are. I'd like your opinion on it, Mr. Brown.

PADDINGTON   It doesn't seem to be one thing or the other.

MR. GRUBER   Ah! It isn't at the moment. But just you wait until I've cleaned it! I gave five shillings[2] for that painting years and years ago, when it was just a picture of a sailing ship. And what do you think? When I started to clean it the other day, all the paint began to come off and I discovered that there was another painting underneath. [*confidentially*] It could be an old master.

---

[2]shillings: about twenty-five cents in United States currency

PADDINGTON   An old master? It looks like an old lady to me.

MR. GRUBER   [*laughs*] What I mean is, it could be very valuable. It could be by a famous painter.

PADDINGTON   That sounds interesting. Very interesting indeed. [*He gets up, his mind obviously elsewhere.*] I'll have to be going now, Mr. Gruber. Thank you for the elevenses.

MR. GRUBER   Is anything the matter, Mr. Brown?

PADDINGTON   No, Mr. Gruber. I've had an idea, that's all. [*mysteriously, as he makes to leave*] I may come into some money soon.

MR. GRUBER   Good day, Mr. Brown. I shall look forward to that. [*He watches* PADDINGTON *go.*] Come into some money! I wonder what he meant by that?

Scene Three

[*The Browns' sitting room.* PADDINGTON *comes in, looks round carefully. He takes a bottle of paint remover from his coat pocket. He soaks a handkerchief in paint remover and rubs it over the painting. He stands back to look and, horrified by what he sees, decides to have another try. He is giving the painting a vigorous scrub when* MRS. BIRD *enters.*]

MRS. BIRD   Now, Paddington, what are you up to? I thought you were out shopping.

PADDINGTON   I was. But I'm not any more. [*gloomily*] I wish I still was.

MRS. BIRD   Whatever's the matter? [*She sees the picture.*] What *have* you been doing? That's the painting Mr. Brown did specially for the exhibition.

PADDINGTON   I know. I thought there might be an old master underneath.

MRS. BIRD   An old master? [*She looks at the painting.*] It used to be some boats on a lake. It looks more like a storm at sea now. He'll be most upset when he sees it.

PADDINGTON   I know, Mrs. Bird. What can I do?

MRS. BIRD   They're coming to collect it today. There's only one hope. Perhaps you could touch it up before they get here.

PADDINGTON   That's a good idea, Mrs. Bird. Except I haven't any paints.

MRS. BIRD   There's an old box under the stairs. I'll get them for you. [*She goes.*]

PADDINGTON   I wonder if it will work. [*He gets a jar of marmalade, takes a spoonful, and then puts it on the table near the easel.*]

MRS. BIRD   [*coming in with a paintbox and palette*] Here we are. It's very old, but it's the best I can do.

PADDINGTON   Thank you, Mrs. Bird.

MRS. BIRD   I hope you manage something. I don't know, I'm sure . . .

[*She goes to the kitchen.*]

PADDINGTON   [*Holding the brush at arm's length, he considers the canvas.*] Uh, huh. [*He squeezes a tube of red paint on the palette, then he does the same with a green tube. He begins to paint boldly. Although we can't see the painting, it is obvious that he is making a mess.*] That looks better! [*Throughout this painting scene* PADDINGTON *occasionally touches the brush to his face, without realizing he is giving himself red and green spots. He dabs at the painting, absent-mindedly dipping his brush into the marmalade, and then decides to experiment. First he adds some mustard, and then the contents of a washing-up liquid squeezer and a bottle of tomato ketchup.*] There's one thing about painting, it's fun. [*He makes a huge mess of it.* MISS BLACK *arrives to collect the picture and knocks at the front door.* PADDINGTON *puts down his brush and goes to the door.*]

MISS BLACK   Good afternoon. I believe Mr. Brown has a painting for our exhibition.

PADDINGTON   Oh, yes. That's right. I'll get it for you. [*He goes back, gives the painting a finishing dab, wipes the brush on his hat, and takes the painting to the front door.*]

MISS BLACK   Thank you very much. The final judging takes place this afternoon.

PADDINGTON   The *final* judging?

MISS BLACK   Yes, we shall be awarding the prizes today. I expect you will hear the results later this evening. Goodbye. [*She goes.*]

PADDINGTON   Goodbye. There's something else about painting—it's fun while it lasts, but it's much more difficult than it looks. I can't think what Mr. Brown will say . . .

248

Scene Four

[*Later that day. The* BROWN *family is in the sitting room after dinner.*]

MRS. BROWN   Would you like a cup of cocoa,
Paddington?
PADDINGTON   No, thank you.
MRS. BROWN   Are you all right?

PADDINGTON   Yes, I thank so, think you. I mean, I think so, thank you.

MRS. BROWN   Nothing on your mind?

PADDINGTON   No.

JONATHAN   How about a bull's-eye?[3]

PADDINGTON   No, thank you. I think I'll just go and have a rest for a bit. [*He goes out of the room.*]

MRS. BROWN   I do hope he's all right, Henry. He hardly touched his dinner, and that's not like him at all. And he seemed to have some funny red spots all over his face.

JONATHAN   Red spots! I wonder if it's measles. I hope he's given it to me, whatever it is. Then I will be able to stay away from school.

JUDY   Well, he's got green ones as well. I distinctly saw them.

MR. BROWN   Green ones! I wonder if he's sickening for something? If they're not gone in the morning, we'd better send for the doctor.

JONATHAN   They're judging the paintings today, aren't they, Dad?

MR. BROWN   Yes, they took mine away this afternoon.

JONATHAN   Do you think you'll win a prize?

MRS. BROWN   No one will be more surprised than your father if he does. He's never won a prize yet.

MR. BROWN   It took me a long while but I don't suppose I'll be any luckier than last time. The lady who collected it this afternoon told Paddington that the results would be made known today, so we'll soon know.

---

[3]bull's-eye: very hard round candy

JUDY   I wonder if he's feeling
   any better? [*She goes out.*]
JONATHAN   Perhaps they have
   green measles in Darkest Peru.

[*There is a knock at the front door.
   MRS. BIRD goes to answer it.*]

MRS. BIRD   Who can that be?

[*MRS. BIRD opens the door. MISS
   BLACK is waiting outside. She has
   a MAN with her. He is carrying Mr.
   Brown's painting, still with its back to the audience.*]

MISS BLACK   Good evening. Is Mr. Brown in?
MAN   We've come about the painting he
   entered for our competition.
MRS. BIRD   Oh, dear. Will you come
   this way, please? [*She ushers them
   into the room.*]
MAN   Mr. Brown?
MR. BROWN   That's right.
MAN   I'm the President of the Art
   Society, and this is Miss Black, who was
   one of the judges of the competition.
MR. BROWN   How do you do.
MAN   I've some news for you, Mr. Brown.
PADDINGTON   [*offstage*] Oooooh!
MISS BLACK   Good gracious! What was that?
MAN   It sounded like a cow mooing somewhere.
MRS. BROWN   I think it's only a bear oooohing.

MAN   Oh! Er . . . Mr. Brown, as I was saying,
the judges decided that your painting was most
unusual . . .

MRS. BIRD   It certainly was.

MAN   And they have all agreed to award you the first
prize.

MR. BROWN   The *first* prize?

MISS BLACK   Yes, they thought your painting showed
great imagination.

MR. BROWN   [*pleased*] Did they now?

MAN   It made great use of marmalade chunks.

THE BROWNS   [*chorus*] Marmalade chunks!

MAN   Yes, indeed. I don't think I've ever come across
anything quite like it before. [*He places the painting on
the easel facing the audience. It is, to say the least, unusual,
and there are several real marmalade chunks sticking to it.*]

MRS. BROWN   I didn't know you were interested in
abstract art, Henry.

MR. BROWN   Nor did I!

[PADDINGTON *and* JUDY *put their heads round the door.*]

MAN   [*He removes a marmalade chunk with a flourish and
swallows it.*] It not only looks good—it tastes good!

MISS BLACK   What are you calling it?

MR. BROWN   Where's Paddington?

MISS BLACK   Where's Paddington? What a funny title!

MAN   Well, sir, my congratulations! We'll be wanting
the painting back in a day or so to put into the
exhibition, but I'll leave it with you for the moment.
Just one more thing . . . your prize. [*He hands over a
cheque.*] £10.[4]

---

[4]£10: 10 pounds; about twenty American dollars

MISS BLACK   May I ask what you will do with it, Mr. Brown?

MR. BROWN   [*wearily*] I think perhaps I'd better give it to a certain Home for Retired Bears in South America.

MAN   Oh, really? Well, we must be getting along.

[*As they leave,* PADDINGTON *falls into the room.* JUDY *follows him in.*]

MRS. BIRD   Well, Paddington. The secret's out. Now, what have you got to say for yourself?

PADDINGTON   [*Crosses to the painting. He removes a marmalade chunk and goes to eat it.*] I think it looks good enough to eat, Mr. Brown! [*He turns it up the other way.*] But I think they might have put it the right way up. After all, it's not every day a bear wins first prize in a painting competition.

CURTAIN

THINK IT OVER

1. Why did Paddington change Mr. Brown's painting? What did he do to try to correct his mistake?

2. Why did Mr. Brown's painting win first prize?

3. Why was Paddington acting so strangely after dinner?

4. If you were one of the judges, how would you have rated Paddington's painting? Explain why.

WRITE

Think about the adventures Paddington had. Write a list of other adventures Paddington could have for a new scene.

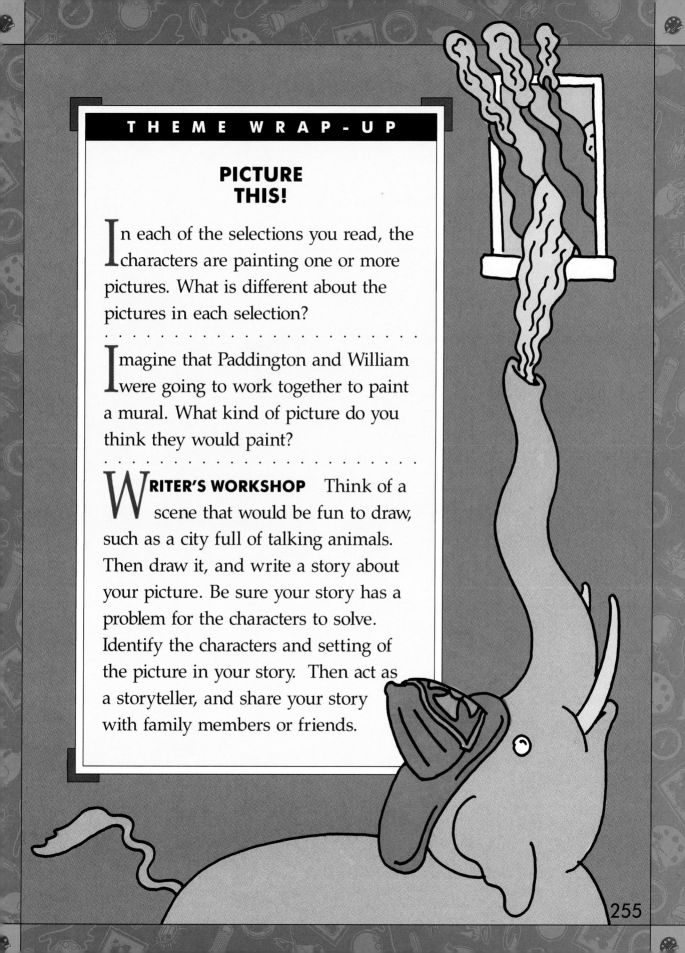

PICTURE THIS!

In each of the selections you read, the characters are painting one or more pictures. What is different about the pictures in each selection?

. . . .

Imagine that Paddington and William were going to work together to paint a mural. What kind of picture do you think they would paint?

. . . .

WRITER'S WORKSHOP Think of a scene that would be fun to draw, such as a city full of talking animals. Then draw it, and write a story about your picture. Be sure your story has a problem for the characters to solve. Identify the characters and setting of the picture in your story. Then act as a storyteller, and share your story with family members or friends.

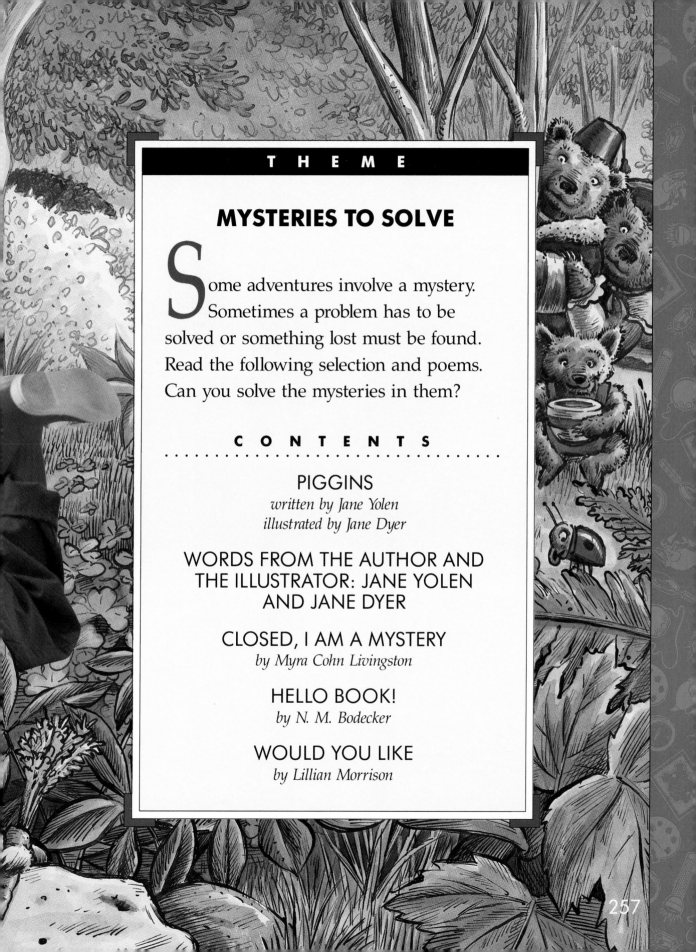

MYSTERIES TO SOLVE

Some adventures involve a mystery. Sometimes a problem has to be solved or something lost must be found. Read the following selection and poems. Can you solve the mysteries in them?

C O N T E N T S

Trit-trot, trit-trot.

That is the sound of Piggins, the butler at 47 The Meadows, going up the stairs. He has shined the silver teapot so well he can see his snout in it.

UPSTAIRS Mrs. Reynard is in a terrible dither.

"I cannot find my diamond lavaliere," she says to her husband.

"Is it missing again?" Mr. Reynard asks. "Perhaps one of the servants took it." His whiskers twitch.

"*Our* Cook? *Our* Sara? *Our* Jane? Not possible," says Mrs. Reynard.

Mr. Reynard smiles widely enough so that his teeth show. "Perhaps the butler did it."

"*Our* Piggins?" Mrs. Reynard is clearly shocked. "He *finds* things. He does not *take* things."

"I know, my dear," says Mr. Reynard. "I was making a little joke. Look again and I will help you." He gets up from his chair.

They look and look. At last they find the necklace right where it belongs—in Mrs. Reynard's jewelry box.

ILLUSTRATED BY JANE DYER

BELOW STAIRS Cook has just removed the cake from the oven. The kitchen is sweet with its smell. Sara, the scullery maid, has scrubbed the pots and pans. She looks as if she needs a scrubbing herself. Upstairs Jane has finished setting the table. Everything is in its proper place.

IN THE DINING ROOM Piggins is pleased. The glasses sparkle. The silver gleams. Even the chandelier glitters like a thousand diamonds.

Ding-dong. That is the front door bell. Piggins goes to answer it. The dinner guests have started to arrive.

Inspector Bayswater and his friend Professor T. Ortoise are on the steps. The professor is telling a joke. Lord and Lady Ratsby alight from a carriage. They are arguing with the driver over the fare. Down the street comes the motorcar of the world-famous explorer Pierre Lapin and his three unmarried sisters. He honks the horn. *Aaaa-OOOO-ga. Aaaa-OOOO-ga.* His sisters scream with delight.

"Lovely weather," says the professor in the living room. He is famous for his conversation. His students all say proudly, "Professor T. Ortoise taught us."

Lord and Lady Ratsby eye the cheeses hungrily. They sample every cheese and even slip a few pieces into their pockets.

Inspector Bayswater takes out his pipe. He does not light it. The doctors have advised him not to smoke.

Pierre Lapin settles his sisters. "Do you want something to drink?" he asks them.

"Anything but tea," the eldest says. The other two giggle.

Mr. and Mrs. Reynard come into the room and smile warmly at their friends. They greet each of them by name. Everyone admires Mrs. Reynard's diamond lavaliere.

"You may wonder why I have asked you here this evening," says Mr. Reynard.

But no one *really* wonders. Mr. Reynard is a tinkerer. He loves to invite friends over to show off his latest invention.

Mr. Reynard surprises them. "Tonight I will say nothing about my inventions, though I do have one or two small new things." He waves his paw toward several strange contraptions in the corner of the room. "Tonight I want to tell you about—"

"Dinner is served," announces Piggins.

So two by two they go in to dinner. Lord and Lady Ratsby are so hungry they scamper on ahead. Slow but steady, the professor brings up the rear, the eldest Miss Lapin on his arm. It would simply not do to let Cook's wonderful food get cold.

When the shrimp soup has been served, Mr. Reynard smiles. "I have invited you to dinner tonight so that you can admire my wife's brand-new diamond necklace. And so you can hear the story of why we must sell it."

"Sell it?" The eldest Miss Lapin leans forward. "But it is so beautiful. How can you bear to part with it?"

"It must be worth a great deal of money," says Lady Ratsby. She fingers her own necklace, a simple gold chain.

"Yes, it *is* beautiful," says Mrs. Reynard. "And quite expensive. But . . . "

"But what?" asks the inspector. His professional interest has been aroused.

"There is a curse on the diamond!" says Mr. Reynard.

"A curse!" Everyone talks at once.

Mr. Reynard silences them by holding up his right paw. "Yes—a curse! The miner who found the diamond broke his arm. The cutter who shaped it broke all his tools. The store that sold the necklace burned down right after the sale."

"And you?" asks the professor, keeping the conversation going.

"Yes," says Pierre Lapin. "What has happened to you?"

Mrs. Reynard looks sad. "I have lost the lavaliere three times already. Sara broke a bowl and a glass. Cook's first cake flopped. The children have the fox pox. And—"

"Nothing serious has happened . . . yet," says Mr. Reynard. "But just in case, we have decided to sell the lavaliere as soon as possible. I know all of you are interested in gems, so I called you together tonight."

"We are interested indeed," says Lord Ratsby. *"What good timing!"*

Suddenly the lights go out.

A strange tinkling sound is heard.

There is a scramble of feet.

Several objects thud to the floor.

There is a high, squeaky scream.

In comes Piggins with a candle.

Lord Ratsby finds the light switch and turns on the glittering chandelier.

Professor T. Ortoise stands up.

Pierre Lapin sets the table aright.

Just then Mrs. Reynard clutches her throat. She screams.

"My diamond lavaliere. It is gone." She falls back in a faint.

Lady Ratsby points her finger at Piggins. "Perhaps the butler did it."

"Balderdash and poppycock," says Mr. Reynard. He turns to the inspector. "I cannot believe *our* Piggins did it. Can you find any clues to the real thief?"

The inspector examines the room. He searches everywhere. He finds a red thread near the door, crumbs on the table, and a little bit of dirt on the floor. He cannot find the diamond lavaliere.

"I am stumped," he says at last.

"Hummmmph!" snorts Lady Ratsby.

Professor T. Ortoise is at a loss for words for the first time in his life.

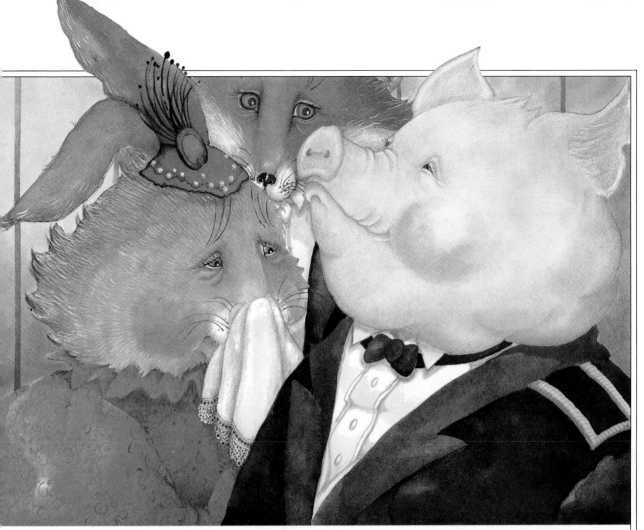

Pierre Lapin comforts his three sisters, who sniffle into their lace handkerchiefs.

Mrs. Reynard comes out of her faint.

Piggins smiles. "I, on the other hand, am not stumped. I know who has done it."

"Good show, Piggins," says Mr. Reynard. "Tell us everything. And I will record it with my latest invention."

"First there are the clues," says Piggins. "A piece of red thread near the door. A trail of cheese crumbs on the table. The tinkling sound we all heard. The scream."

"And the dirt on the floor?" asks the inspector.

"For that I shall have to speak sharply to Upstairs Jane," says Piggins, frowning. "There should be *no* dirt in this house."

"I do not understand the clues," says the professor. "Thread, crumbs, a tinkling sound, a scream."

"There is not one thief—but two," explains Piggins. "One to turn off the lights and make a commotion, and one to steal the diamond lavaliere."

"Oh," says Pierre Lapin. "I know all about making commotions. In my youth, I stole into a farmer's garden and made much too much noise."

"The clues," remind the Misses Lapin together.

Piggins continues. "Before everyone came into dinner, someone tied the red thread to the light switch. At a signal, the thread was pulled and the lights turned off. But the thread was pulled so hard, it broke. In the dark someone grabbed the necklace and stepped up onto the table, leaving a trail of cheese crumbs where no cheese had been served. The tinkling sound was the chandelier being disturbed. The scream was the signal that all was clear."

"Then that means . . . " says Inspector Bayswater.

"That the thieves are . . . " says the professor.

"None other than . . . " says Mr. Reynard.

"Lord and Lady Ratsby," finishes Piggins. "They knew about the diamond all along and planned to steal it at their very first chance."

"But where *is* the diamond?" asks the professor. "Inspector Bayswater looked everywhere."

"Yes," sneers Lord Ratsby. "Where is your precious diamond?"

Piggins smiles. "In plain sight." He steps on one of the chairs and reaches up into the glittering chandelier. He finds the necklace.

"I suspected the Ratsbys were broke," says the eldest Miss Lapin. "Lady Ratsby is wearing a simple gold chain. Usually she drips jewels."

"Catch them!" Mrs. Reynard cries, for the Ratsbys are trying to escape.

The eldest Miss Lapin sticks out her foot. She trips Lord Ratsby. The younger Misses Lapin jump on top of Lady Ratsby.

"Well done, Piggins," says Mr. Reynard.

"Well done, girls!" cries Mrs. Reynard.

"Curses!" says Lord Ratsby.

Professor T. Ortoise laughs. "Curses indeed! Perhaps, Reynard, the curse on your lavaliere is at its end."

The police are summoned and they take the Ratsbys away.

UPSTAIRS Mr. and Mrs. Reynard get ready for bed. Mrs. Reynard carefully wraps the diamond lavaliere in a velvet cloth. She puts it away in her jewelry box. "I hope the curse *is* ended," she says. "I would hate to part with my beautiful necklace."

Mr. Reynard nods and takes off his tie. "I knew the butler did not do it," he says.

"Not *our* Piggins," says Mrs. Reynard.

BELOW STAIRS Sara has cleaned the last of the dishes. She could do with a cleaning herself. Cook snoozes in her chair. And Jane, having swept up the dirt on the dining room floor, has set the kettle on the stove for one last cup of tea.

IN THE DINING ROOM Everything is quiet and clean. Piggins locks the front door at 47 The Meadows. He hears the kettle whistling.

It has been a long and interesting evening. Piggins is tired. Teapot in hand, he goes back down the stairs. *Trit-trot, trit-trot, trit-trot.*

THINK IT OVER

1. How did Piggins solve the mystery?

2. Who prevented the thieves from getting away?

3. Why didn't Mr. and Mrs. Reynard suspect Piggins of being the thief?

4. When in the story did you know who took the necklace? Tell how you knew.

WRITE

Think about another mystery story you have heard, seen, or read. What does it have in common with the Piggins story? Write a paragraph comparing them.

WORDS FROM THE
AUTHOR *And The* ILLUSTRATOR:

AWARD-WINNING
AUTHOR

Jane Yolen and Jane Dyer

Every story has a starting place, but it is often difficult to guess it. You may think that *Piggins* began with *Trit-trot, trit-trot* but actually it began with a series of mystery books, a television show, and an illustration of three bears.

The series of mystery books I mean were from England and star a detective named Lord Peter Wimsey. His butler, Bunter, assists him in every mystery he solves. Written in the 1930s and 1940s by British author Dorothy Sayers, these books are particular favorites of mine, and I have read each of them many times.

The television show is a long-running series called *Upstairs, Downstairs*. It's about a British family in the late 1800s and early 1900s. The family has a butler, a cook, a messy young kitchen maid, an upstairs maid, and a house with a great many rooms. They are always holding formal dinner parties.

The illustration was shown to me during a writing class I was teaching. The young artist, Jane Dyer, had done work for textbooks and sticker books, but she had never illustrated a picture book before. I fell in love with one illustration showing three bears sitting down to a breakfast of porridge. They were elegantly dressed in their cozy little forest cottage.

Without really meaning to, I came up with an idea for a book: What about a . . . a pig butler named Piggins, dressed in a tuxedo, who works for a family in a fancy house and solves mysteries? When I asked Jane Dyer if she would like to try the illustrations she looked at me as if I were crazy.

"Would I?" she whispered in a soft voice. Then she almost shouted, "Oh, boy, WOULD I!"

And she did.

P.S. Here is a funny ending to the story. Four years after the first of the three PIGGINS books came out, I got a letter from a lady named Mrs. Ethel Piggins. She wondered if I had heard of her and if her name had given me the idea for my books. She said that I had met her daughter once years before. I didn't remember meeting her daughter and told her so. Several months later a young woman named Ms. Reynard asked me the same question. I hadn't ever met her before either. But sometimes the things you make up come true— in an odd sort of way.

Closed, I am a mystery

by Myra Cohn Livingston

Closed, I am a mystery.
Open, I will always be
a friend with whom you think and see.

Closed, there's nothing I can say.
Open, we can dream and stray
to other worlds, far and away.

(A BOOK)

Hello Book!

by N.M. Bodecker

illustrated by Merle Nacht

Hello book!
What are you up to?
Keeping yourself to yourself,
shut in between your covers,
a prisoner high on a shelf.
Come in book!
What is your story?
Haven't you ever been read?
Did you think
    I would just pass by you,
And pick me a comic instead?
No way book!
I'm your reader.
I open you up. Set you free.
Listen, I know a secret!
Will you share
    your secrets with me?

Would you like

by Lillian Morrison

illustrated by Michael Stiernagle

stories that surprise you
and/or hypnotize you,
a mystery, a history,
a volume to advise you
how to fix a motor,
build your own computer,
use a tape recorder,
get along with mother?
How about a voyage
into outer space,
romance with an Alien
of a future race?
Then dip in, dig in
grapple in with hooks,
dive in, delve in
GET INTO BOOKS.

MYSTERIES
TO
SOLVE

Based on what you read in "Piggins," what qualities do you think would help someone solve a mystery?

. . . .

The poems you read are about books. How can books be mysteries? Explain your answer.

. . . .

WRITER'S WORKSHOP Write a descriptive paragraph for a newspaper advertisement to sell Mrs. Reynard's necklace. Be sure to describe the necklace in detail and include the price in your ad.

Fox Gazette

Missing
Necklace
Found

GONE CAMPING

Much of your time is spent with friends, classmates, and family members. Some adventures occur with people you see and hear every day. Read the following family adventure and poems. Does anything sound familiar?

C O N T E N T S

AWARD-WINNING
AUTHOR AND
ILLUSTRATOR

THE LOST LAKE

ALLEN SAY

I went to live with Dad last summer.

Every day he worked in his room from morning to
night, sometimes on weekends, too. Dad wasn't much
of a talker, but when he was busy he didn't talk at all.

I didn't know anybody in the city, so I stayed
home most of the time. It was too hot to play outside
anyway. In one month I finished all the books I'd
brought and grew tired of watching TV.

One morning I started cutting pictures out of old

magazines, just to be doing something. They were pictures of mountains and rivers and lakes, and some showed people fishing and canoeing. Looking at them made me feel cool, so I pinned them up in my room.

Dad didn't notice them for two days. When he did, he looked at them one by one.

"Nice pictures," he said.

"Are you angry with me, Dad?" I asked, because he saved old magazines for his work.

"It's all right, Luke," he said. "I'm having this place painted soon anyway."

He thought I was talking about the marks I'd made on the wall.

That Saturday Dad woke me up early in the morning and told me we were going camping! I was wide awake in a second. He gave me a pair of brand-new hiking boots to try out. They were perfect.

In the hallway I saw a big backpack and a knapsack all packed and ready to go.

"What's in them, Dad?" I asked.

"Later," he said. "We have a long drive ahead of us."

In the car I didn't ask any more questions because Dad was so grumpy in the morning.

"Want a sip?" he said, handing me his mug. He'd never let me drink coffee before. It had lots of sugar in it.

"Where are we going?" I finally asked.

"We're off to the Lost Lake, my lad."

"How can you lose a lake?"

"No one's found it, that's how." Dad was smiling! "Grandpa and I used to go there a long time ago. It was our special place, so don't tell any of your friends."

"I'll never tell," I promised. "How long are we going to stay there?"

"Five days, maybe a week."

"We're going to sleep outside for a whole week?"

"That's the idea."

"Oh, boy!"

We got to the mountains in the afternoon.

"It's a bit of a hike to the lake, son," Dad said.

"I don't mind," I told him. "Are there any fish in the lake?"

"Hope so. We'll have to catch our dinner, you know."

"You didn't bring any food?"

"Of course not. We're going to live like true outdoorsmen."

"Oh . . ."

Dad saw my face and started to laugh. He must have been joking. I didn't think we were going very far anyway, because Dad's pack was so heavy I couldn't even lift it.

Well, Dad was like a mountain goat. He went straight up the trail, whistling all the while. But I was gasping in no time. My knapsack got very heavy and I started to fall behind.

Dad stopped for me often, but he wouldn't let me take off my pack. If I did I'd be too tired to go on, he said.

It was almost suppertime when we got to the lake.

The place reminded me of the park near Dad's apartment. He wasn't whistling or humming anymore.

"Welcome to the *Found* Lake," he muttered from the side of his mouth.

"What's wrong, Dad?"

"Do you want to camp with all these people around us?"

"I don't mind."

"Well, I do!"

"Are we going home?"

"Of course not!"

He didn't even take off his pack. He just turned and started to walk away.

Soon the lake was far out of sight.

Then it started to rain. Dad gave me a poncho and

it kept me dry, but I wondered where we were going to sleep that night. I wondered what we were going to do for dinner. I wasn't sure about camping anymore.

I was glad when Dad finally stopped and set up the tent. The rain and wind beat against it, but we were warm and cozy inside. And Dad had brought food. For dinner we had salami and dried apricots.

"I'm sorry about the lake, Dad," I said.

He shook his head. "You know something, Luke? There aren't any secret places left in the world anymore."

"What if we go very far up in the mountains? Maybe we can find our own lake."

"There are lots of lakes up here, but that one was special."

"But we've got a whole week, Dad."

"Well, why not? Maybe we'll find a lake that's not on the map."

"Sure, we will!"

We started early in the morning. When the fog cleared we saw other hikers ahead of us. Sure enough, Dad became very glum.

"We're going cross-country, partner," he said.

"Won't we get lost?"

"A wise man never leaves home without his compass."

So we went off the trail. The hills went on and on. The mountains went on and on. It was kind of lonesome. It seemed as if Dad and I were the only people left in the world.

And then we hiked into a big forest.

At noontime we stopped by a creek and ate lunch
and drank ice-cold water straight from the stream. I
threw rocks in the water, and fish, like shadows,
darted in the pools.

"Isn't this a good place to camp, Dad?"

"I thought we were looking for our lake."

"Yes, right . . ." I mumbled.

The forest went on and on.

"I don't mean to scare you, son," Dad said. "But
we're in bear country. We don't want to surprise them,

so we have to make a lot of noise. If they hear us, they'll just go away."

What a time to tell me! I started to shout as loudly as I could. Even Dad wouldn't be able to beat off bears. I thought about those people having fun back at the lake. I thought about the creek, too, with all those fish in it. That would have been a fine place to camp. The Lost Lake hadn't been so bad either.

It was dark when we got out of the forest. We built a fire and that made me feel better. Wild animals wouldn't come near a fire. Dad cooked beef stroganoff and it was delicious.

Later it was bedtime. The sleeping bag felt wonderful. Dad and I started to count the shooting stars, then I worried that maybe we weren't going to find our lake.

"What are you thinking about, Luke?" Dad asked.

"I didn't know you could cook like that," I said.

Dad laughed. "That was only freeze-dried stuff. When we get home, I'll cook you something really special."

"You know something, Dad? You seem like a different person up here."

"Better or worse?"

"A lot better."

"How so?"

"You talk more."

"I'll have to talk more often, then."

That made me smile. Then I slept.

Dad shook me awake. The sun was just coming up, turning everything all gold and orange and yellow. And there was the lake, right in front of us.

For a long time we watched the light change on the water, getting brighter and brighter. Dad didn't say a word the whole time. But then, I didn't have anything to say either.

After breakfast we climbed a mountain and saw our lake below us. There wasn't a sign of people anywhere. It really seemed as if Dad and I were all alone in the world.

I liked it just fine.

THINK IT OVER

1. Why did Luke's father seem like a different person at the end of the story?

2. Luke was happy that his father talked more when they went hiking. Why didn't Luke mind that they were silent when they looked out on the lake at the end of the story?

3. Would you have liked to go on the camping trip with Luke and his father? Explain why or why not.

WRITE

Luke had several disappointments while camping. Do you think he had a good or bad vacation? Write a post-card that Luke might have sent to a friend, telling how he felt about the trip.

Words from the AUTHOR and ILLUSTRATOR:

Allen Say

I began *Lost Lake* by painting the pictures. I didn't really know what the story was going to be about until I was halfway through the art. This is how I work. I find my characters through the pictures. When the characters I'm drawing become real to me, then the story starts to take shape.

293

I had actually gone to a place called Lost Lake in my twenties when I came out of the army. A friend, who was a very outdoorsy person, took me there. I had done a lot of camping when I was in the army, so I wasn't very keen to go to this place in the Sierra Mountains, but I went with my friend. We had to trek six miles before we got to Lost Lake, and just as in the story, the area was full of people with radios and dirt bikes. It was noisy! I remembered that incident, and it became the kernel of the text.

I also wanted to write about the kind of father I wished I had had, but when I finished the story, I suddenly realized that the father in it is me. Maybe this was my way of apologizing to my daughter, because I didn't feel I was spending enough time with her. So, like my other stories, this one became very personal.

It can take a long time to do a picture book. One book, *El Chino*, took me eleven months to write, and during that period I had only one weekend off.

Although I haven't done it in a while, when I need time off in a quiet place, I go fly-fishing. I've fished in Iceland, Alaska, and Argentina. Now, because I'm so busy, I don't really have an outdoors life. I have to be content with taking walks.

PEOPLE

by Charlotte Zolotow
illustrated by Andrea Eberbach

Some people talk and talk
and never say a thing.
Some people look at you
and birds begin to sing.

Some people laugh and laugh
and yet you want to cry.
Some people touch your hand
and music fills the sky.

Some PEOPLE

by Rachel Field
illustrated by
Andrea Eberbach

Isn't it strange some people make
　　You feel so tired inside,
Your thoughts begin to shrivel up
　　Like leaves all brown and dried!

But when you're with some other ones,
　　It's stranger still to find
Your thoughts as thick as fireflies
　　All shiny in your mind!

GONE CAMPING

In "The Lost Lake," the camping trip doesn't turn out as planned. Which character, Luke or his father, do you think enjoys himself more? Tell why you think as you do.

. . . .

People and the way they act are important in the selections you read. Compare and contrast Luke's father with the characters in the poems.

. . . .

WRITER'S WORKSHOP   Write a paragraph telling how families can have a good time on a camping trip or other vacation. Be sure to include some directions for avoiding danger or problems. For example, you might want to write about how to stay safe while swimming. Remember to use exact words in your directions.

SKUNK CROSSING

CONNECTIONS

Paul Sierra

SIERRA'S MYSTERY PICTURE

Look at the man in the painting. Who could he be? What is happening all around him? What might he do next?

Paul Sierra, the Chicago artist who painted this picture, has presented us with a mystery. We do not know where this scene is set. Could it show something that happened in Cuba, where the artist grew up?

We can't be sure. Only Sierra knows the answer, and he does not tell us. Like most artists, he wants his work to touch our feelings and make us think. Any thought or feeling we have about the picture is as right as any other.

■ Paint a picture that creates a mood of mystery and adventure. Ask your classmates what your picture makes them think and feel.

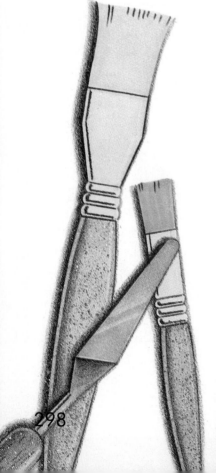

298

THE MYSTERIES OF MEMORY

Paul Sierra grew up in Cuba. Look at photographs of Cuba or another Caribbean island, and read about that place. Imagine that you are an artist from that island. Describe some memories that you would paint.

A PLACE LIKE NO OTHER

What plants might be in the scene that Paul Sierra painted? Draw or map an imaginary island where your favorite unusual or useful plants grow. Write captions that tell why you like these plants.

A chart like this might help you make choices.

Name of Plant	How It Is Unusual or Useful

Handbook
for
Readers and Writers

ACTIVE READING STRATEGIES

A strategy is a plan for doing something successfully. Most of the time you do not even think about the strategies you use when you are reading. But even good readers can become better by thinking about strategies. You can do this by asking yourself questions.

Megan has been learning how to use some strategies by asking herself questions before, during, and after she reads.

Before reading, Megan

✓ **previews**, or looks quickly through, what she is about to read.

> *Does this look packed with information? Are there lots of pictures?*

✓ **thinks of what she already knows** about the topic.

> *Does anything here remind me of something I know or have done?*

✓ **predicts** what the selection is about.

> *What do I think I will learn? What happens to the characters in the story?*

✓ thinks about her **purpose** for reading.

> *What am I going to read to find out?*

During reading, Megan

✓ **pictures** in her mind what she is reading.

> *How would this look if I really saw it in front of me?*

✓ **stops** once in a while to ask herself how she is doing.

> *Do I know that hard word? Can I understand the paragraph without knowing? If not, how can I figure it out?*

> *Does what I predicted seem to be happening? If not, how should I change my prediction?*

> *Do I understand this? If not, what can I do to help myself understand it?*

After reading, Megan

✓ thinks back to her **purpose** for reading.

✓ tells herself **what she learned** so that she can remember it better.

✓ decides whether she wants to read more about **the same topic** or other things written **by the same author.**

> *Did I find out what I thought I would?*

> *What did I learn that I didn't know before?*

> *I could tell a friend how much I liked the book.*

READING FICTION

Fiction is writing that tells a story an author has made up. Follow Luis as he begins to read the fiction story "Miss Rumphius." You'll see how he uses some reading strategies **before** and **during** his reading.

Before I read the story, I'll look at the pictures. I remember seeing ships like the ones in this picture in a movie on TV.

From looking at the picture and the story title, I want to find out who Miss Rumphius is and what she did when she was a little girl.

I can picture how these flowers and rocks would look.

Now I realize that Miss Rumphius, the Lupine Lady, and Alice are all the same person. I hope the story will tell me why she is called the Lupine Lady.

I don't know what a figurehead is. Maybe it doesn't matter. As I continue to read, I learn that her grandfather is an artist.

Miss Rumphius

by Barbara Cooney

The Lupine Lady lives in a small house overlooking the sea. In between the rocks around her house grow blue and purple and rose-colored flowers. The Lupine Lady is little and old. But she has not always been that way. I know. She is my great-aunt, and she told me so.

Once upon a time she was a little girl named Alice, who lived in a city by the sea. From the front stoop she could see the wharves and the bristling masts of tall ships. Many years ago her grandfather had come to America on a large sailing ship.

Now he worked in the shop at the bottom of the house, making figureheads for the prows of ships, and carving Indians out of wood to put in front of cigar stores. For Alice's grandfather was an artist. He painted pictures, too, of sailing ships and places across the sea. When he was very busy, Alice helped him put in the skies.

This does tell about Miss Rumphius when she was a little girl. I think I'll learn all about her childhood.

In the evening Alice sat on her grandfather's knee and listened to his stories of faraway places. When he had finished, Alice would say, "When I grow up, I too will go to faraway places, and when I grow old, I too will live beside the sea."

"That is all very well, little Alice," said her grandfather, "but there is a third thing you must do."

"What is that?" asked Alice.

"You must do something to make the world more beautiful," said her grandfather.

I wonder what she will do to make the world more beautiful.

"All right," said Alice. But she did not know what that could be.

In the meantime Alice got up and washed her face and ate porridge for breakfast. She went to school and came home and did her homework.

I'm not sure what porridge is. I'll keep reading to see if I need to know.

And pretty soon she was grown up.

Then my Great-aunt Alice set out to do the three things she had told her grandfather she was going to do. She left home and went to live in another city far from the sea and the salt air. There she worked in a library, dusting books and keeping them from getting mixed up, and helping people find the ones they wanted. Some of the books told her about faraway places.

People called her Miss Rumphius now.

But here she is grown up. I'll have to change my prediction that this will be about her childhood. Now I think the rest of the story will tell about Alice after she grew up.

I wonder how Miss Rumphius finally got to live by the sea. Maybe I'll find out as I finish reading the story.

(See pages 16–30 for the entire story of "Miss Rumphius.")

READING NONFICTION

Nonfiction tells facts about real things. Often nonfiction has titles and subtitles to show how the parts are related. It may have charts or diagrams. When you read nonfiction, one strategy you can use is **K-W-L.**

- **K** stands for "What I **K**now." Think about what you already know about the topic. Make a list of things you know.
- **W** stands for "What I **W**ant to Know." Use what you found as you previewed the selection to ask yourself questions you hope to answer as you read.
- **L** stands for "What I **L**earned." After you have finished reading, ask yourself what you learned and whether you learned what you hoped to.

Juan uses this strategy by making a **K-W-L** chart as he reads "A Seed Is a Promise."

What I **K**now	What I **W**ant to Know	What I **L**earned
Plants grow from seeds. A promise is a pledge to do something. Bees and pollen have something to do with flowers.	How could a seed be a promise? What does it promise? How does a plant make seeds?	

First, Juan follows the **K** and **W** steps and makes notes. He thinks about the **W** questions as he reads.

A Seed Is a Promise
by Claire Merrill

You know a lot about seeds.

When you eat an orange, you see little white seeds inside.

You've seen the seeds of other fruits, too—apples, pears, melons, grapes.

Do you know where all these seeds come from? All seeds come from plants.

And in every seed there is a promise, the promise that a new plant will grow.

If you know what kind of plant a seed comes from, you know what it will grow into.

How are seeds made? Most seeds begin inside flowers. Look at the center part of the flower. This is called the pistil. At the bottom of the pistil there are tiny egg cells.

Now look at the parts around the pistil. These are the stamens. They make a yellow powder called pollen.

A grain of pollen must reach an egg cell to make a seed.

Some flowers use their own pollen to make seeds. But most flowers use the pollen of other flowers.

Bees and other insects carry pollen from flower to flower. Wind blows pollen through the air.

A grain of pollen lands on the pistil of a flower. The pollen grain grows a long tube down into the pistil and joins an egg cell. A seed begins.

Soon the flower starts to die. Its petals dry and fall. The flower dies, but inside the pistil new seeds are growing.

Now I know that the author thinks a seed is a promise because a seed promises that a new plant will grow.

This diagram and the explanation help me understand how a plant makes seeds.

I learned that pollen is very important in making seeds. And now I see how the bees help, too.

After Juan read the selection, he took a few minutes to think about what he had learned. He listed the main points in the third column of his chart. What do you think they were?

(See pages 32–37 for the entire selection of "A Seed Is a Promise.")

VOCABULARY STRATEGIES

When you are reading and you meet unfamiliar words, there are a few things you can do. First, decide whether you really need to know the word. Often you will understand the sentence or the paragraph if you simply keep on reading.

If you do need to know the meaning of a word, here are strategies you can use.

- Use **context clues.** You can often find clues in the context, or the words and the sentences around the unfamiliar word.

- Use the **structure** of the word itself. By looking at the parts of the word, you can often figure out how it is related to other words you know.

- If these strategies don't work, you can use a **glossary** or a **dictionary** to find the meaning. If that doesn't help you understand the way the word is used in what you are reading, you can ask someone who might know.

When you figure out an unfamiliar word, it becomes a familiar word. Then it is yours to keep, and you will remember it the next time you read it. Look at the ways context clues and structure help with some words in the paragraphs on the next page.

These three sentences together give you a **context clue** that leads you to the meaning of the word *legumes*.

A person who plants only legumes can have vegetables as well as flowers. Lupines, the beautiful flowers whose seeds were scattered by Miss Rumphius, are a kind of legume. Beans, peas, and peanuts are legumes, too.

Some legumes are annuals, or plants that live only one year and must be replanted the next year. Most of the edible, or eatable, legumes are annuals.

Other legumes are perennials. Perennials are flowering plants that sprout from underground parts every year. They also can grow from seeds.

Sometimes you find a **compound word** made of two words you already know. *Underground* is a compound word that you can figure out easily here.

Sometimes the **definition** of a word is given near it. Here, a definition of *annual* follows the word itself.

A **prefix** can help you figure out a word. *Replanted* is easy when you see that it contains the prefix *re-*, meaning "again."

Sometimes you find a **synonym,** or another word that has the same meaning. *Eatable* is a synonym for *edible* here. Once in a while you might find an **antonym,** or a word that means the opposite, as a clue.

Eatable has a structure clue, too. The **suffix** *-able* tells you that *eatable* means "able to be eaten."

SPEAKING

Many people feel shy about giving a speech or about taking part in a group discussion. You can use strategies to help you feel more comfortable when you speak.

- **Prepare** what you are going to say, especially for a speech or an oral report. In a class discussion, think what you might say before you talk.
- **Practice** if you can. Have a partner listen to your speech and share ideas for making it better.

Kristina and her classmates are sharing ideas about how to improve the first drafts of their personal narratives. As Daniel reads his narrative about planting flowers in a vacant lot, Kristina thinks of an idea that might help him.

She knows that during a class discussion she often doesn't express her ideas clearly. So before she speaks, she takes time to decide what to say and how to say it.

Tomás knows he often speaks too fast. So he practices at home. His sister listens and reminds him to read more slowly and to look back at his paragraph while he practices.

When Tomás reads his paragraph, he pauses after each important word. He speaks loudly enough to be heard.

LISTENING

Did you know there are also strategies for listening? These suggestions can help you be a better listener.

- Decide on a **purpose** for listening by predicting what kinds of things you will hear. You can listen to get directions, to learn information, or just for fun.
- **Pay attention** to what the speaker is saying.
- **Be quiet.** Don't bother the speaker or other listeners.
- **Respond** in a way that fits the event. Clap and laugh at a funny show, but not during a friend's oral report.

Here is how Kristina's and Tomás's audiences listened and responded to them when they spoke.

Daniel's purpose for listening was to get information to improve his personal narrative. He paid attention when Kristina spoke. He thought about what she said and asked himself whether to include her idea. He decided to use it.

The whole class listened to Tomás read his paragraph. Their purpose was to get directions for growing tomatoes for a science project. They were quiet while he read. Afterward, they asked questions to make sure they understood.

THE WRITING PROCESS

The writing process is a strategy that can help you write better. First, you should decide what your **task** is, or the kind of writing you will do. Then think about your **audience** and **purpose.** Your task might be to write a personal narrative. Your purpose might be to entertain an audience of classmates. Now you are ready to move through the stages of the writing process.

PREWRITING

Think of a topic. Ideas can come from your own experiences, books or articles you have read, and things you already know or want to learn more about. You might decide to write about the funny thing that happened during your first swimming race.

Your next step is to organize your ideas. Sometimes just listing the things that happened is enough. Other times you can try a story map, a web, an outline, or a drawing such as this one:

DRAFTING

Begin writing your first draft. Here are some strategies you can use.

- Use your list or drawing to help you write the parts in the right order.
- Get your ideas down on paper. You can make corrections later.

Remember that at the end of each step you can decide either to go to the next step or to start all over again.

RESPONDING AND REVISING

Now, ask your writing partner or group to respond to your first draft. Here are some ideas your partner or group might give you for making your writing better.

- Make the first sentence more interesting.
- Use clearer or more colorful words.
- Cut sentences that don't tell about the topic.

Remember that you do not have to use all their ideas. Change only what you think will make your writing better.

PROOFREADING

After you have made changes, you are ready to correct mistakes. As you proofread, use the editor's marks.

Imagine that the draft shown here about the swimming race is yours. See how you could use editor's marks.

EDITOR'S MARKS	
☰ Use a capital letter.	⟳ Move something.
⊙ Add a period.	~tr Transpose.
∧ Add something.	◯ Spell correctly.
⁀₍,₎ Add a comma.	⊬ Indent paragraph.
˅˅ Add quotation marks.	/ Make a lowercase letter.
✀ Cut something.	⌐ Replace something.

You have not indented this paragraph. Use this mark: ⊬ .

Your partner said *got* wasn't a very colorful word. You agree. Replace it.

⊬ My very first swimming race last summer was funny. I ~~got~~ *climbed* up on the starting block. Then i leaned over and waited for the signal. It went BUZZ! I had never heard it before✀ I was so scared I forgot

---

You should have capitalized the word *I*. Underline it three times like this: ☰ .

Change an exclamation mark to a period by using these marks: ✀⊙.

> swimmers
>
> to dive! All the other (swimers) dived in and raced. Finally, I dived
>
> because
> in. I swam hard. I was last, but I was happy (becuase) everybody
>
> was cheering for me.

Check punctuation. A comma is missing. Use this symbol: $\wedge$.

Circle misspelled words. Write the correct spelling above. Study the word and add it to your own spelling notebook.

PUBLISHING

You are now ready to share your writing with your audience. Check to make sure you have made all the corrections. Copy your work in your best handwriting. Decide how you want to publish it. One way is just to let your audience read it. Here are some other ways.

- Make an audiocassette of yourself reading your narrative aloud, so your audience can listen to it.
- Make a paper-roll "movie" and read your narrative aloud as classmates look at it.
- Invent a board game, using events from your narrative. Introduce the game by reading your paragraph.

THE LIBRARY

A library is a good place to find information. Most libraries are organized in an understandable way.

The **card catalog** can help you find the book you need. Cards describing every book in the library are in drawers. They are in alphabetical order by the first word on the card.

Sometimes a library's card catalog is part of a data base on microfilm or on a computer. There are three ways to find a book in the computerized catalog: by title, by author, and by subject. Suppose you wanted to find books about vegetables. First, type the subject command and the word *vegetables* on the computer keyboard, according to the instructions in the printed guide. The computer will then list titles and **call numbers** of books on the subject of vegetables. Call numbers are on the books and on the library shelves. You can find a book by looking for its call number on the shelf and on the book.

The title card lists the title of the book first.

The author card lists the author's last name first.

The subject card lists the subject of the book first.

Vegetables.
J   Wake, Susan.

635   J   Wake, Susan.
           Vegetables / Susan Wake ;
      635   Illustrated by John Yates.

Vegetables — Juvenile Literature
J   Wake, Susan.
        Vegetables / Susan Wake ;
635   Illustrated by John Yates.
Wak   Minneapolis : Carolrhoda Books,
         Inc., c1989.

THE REFERENCE SECTION

Reference books such as **encyclopedias, dictionaries, almanacs,** and **atlases** are kept in one part of the library. Usually reference books cannot be taken out of the library because so many people need to use them.

An **encyclopedia** is a set of books that gives information about many, many topics. The topics are arranged in alphabetical order. Each volume, or separate book in the encyclopedia, is marked with the letters of the alphabet it includes. If you were looking for information about *vegetables*, you would find it in the volume marked U–V.

A **globe** is a model of the world that shows all the continents, oceans, and countries. A globe is round the way the world is.

An **atlas** is a book of maps. Maps can give more details than a globe can. Maps show capitals of countries, states, or regions. They also show major roads, rivers, and lakes.

An **almanac** gives lists and details about many things including famous people or events. There are many different kinds of almanacs. Most of them are rewritten every year.

Magazines and **newspapers** give the most up-to-date information in the library. These are published every day, week, or month. They help you learn about current events.

GLOSSARY

The **pronunciation** of each word in this glossary is shown by a phonetic respelling in brackets; for example, [ə·fek′shən·it·lē]. An accent mark (′) follows the syllable with the most stress: [an·tēk′]. A secondary, or lighter, accent mark (′) follows a syllable with less stress: [fig′yər·hed′]. The key to other pronunciation symbols is below. You will find a shortened version of this key on alternate pages of the glossary.

Pronunciation Key*

a	add, map	m	move, seem	u	up, done
ā	ace, rate	n	nice, tin	û(r)	burn, term
â(r)	care, air	ng	ring, song	yo͞o	fuse, few
ä	palm, father	o	odd, hot	v	vain, eve
b	bat, rub	ō	open, so	w	win, away
ch	check, catch	ô	order, jaw	y	yet, yearn
d	dog, rod	oi	oil, boy	z	zest, muse
e	end, pet	ou	pout, now	zh	vision, pleasure
ē	equal, tree	o͝o	took, full	ə	the schwa,
f	fit, half	o͞o	pool, food		an unstressed
g	go, log	p	pit, stop		vowel representing
h	hope, hate	r	run, poor		the sound spelled
i	it, give	s	see, pass		a in *above*
ī	ice, write	sh	sure, rush		e in *sicken*
j	joy, ledge	t	talk, sit		i in *possible*
k	cool, take	th	thin, both		o in *melon*
l	look, rule	t̶h̶	this, bathe		u in *circus*

*Adapted entries, the Pronunciation Key, and the Short Key that appear on the following pages are reprinted from *HBJ School Dictionary*. Copyright © 1990 by Harcourt Brace Jovanovich, Inc. Reprinted by permission of Harcourt Brace Jovanovich, Inc.

apricot

A

ab·sent·mind·ed
[ab'sənt·mīn'did] *adj.*
Forgetful; not paying attention: **My *absentminded* uncle often forgets people's birthdays.**

ac·cu·ra·cy [ak'yər·ə·sē] *n.*
Correctness; having no mistakes: **Bruno was known for the *accuracy* of his drawings.**

af·fec·tion·ate·ly
[ə·fek'shən·it·lē] *adv.*
With love and emotion: **The children's mother hugged them *affectionately* when they came home from school.**

an·kle [ang'kəl] *n.* The part of the body that connects the foot and the leg: **Tom's high-top gym shoes came up over his *ankles*.**

an·tique [an·tēk'] *n.* Something made long ago and valued for its age: **The *antiques* in our house are all over a hundred years old.**

a·pri·cot [ā'pri·kot *or* ap'ri·kot] *n.* A small, orange-colored fruit: **Sally ate two *apricots* for a snack.**

athlete

athlete The people who lived in Greece more than 2500 years ago were the first to hold the Olympic Games. They gave prizes to the winners. The word for prize in the ancient Greek language was *athlon*. So an *athlete* was a person who tried to win a prize in a sports contest.

ar·gue [är'gyoo] *v.*
ar·gued, ar·gu·ing To fight by using words: **George and Alice are *arguing* loudly about who will sit in the front seat.** *syn.* disagree

as·sign [ə·sīn'] *v.*
as·signed, as·sign·ing To give someone a job or task to do: **The teacher *assigned* homework today.**

as·sur·ance [ə·shoor'əns] *n.* Words or actions that make someone feel better or less afraid: **The child needed *assurance* that he was safe during the storm.**

ath·lete [ath'lēt'] *n.* A person who is very good in sports: **An *athlete* who takes part in the Olympic games is one of the best in the world.**

B

base·ment [bās'mənt] *n.* The lowest floor of a house or building, partly below ground level: **We ran down into the *basement* when we heard the tornado warning.**

beck·on [bek′ən]
v. **beck·oned,
beck·on·ing** To signal or
call to come over: **The
teacher waved and** *beckoned* **the students into
the classroom.**

bois·ter·ous [bois′tər·əs]
adj. Noisy and wild: **The**
boisterous **children in
the yard made it hard to
hear the TV.** *syns.* loud,
excited

bound [bound] *v.*
bound·ed, bound·ing
To leap: **We saw the
playful orange kitten**
bounding **toward the
fallen leaf.**

Braille [brāl] *n.* A system
of writing for people
who are blind that uses
raised dots as letters and
numbers to be read with
the fingertips: **Instead of
using their eyes to read
printing, people who are
blind use their fingers to
read** *Braille.*

bribe [brīb] *v.* To give
someone something so
they will do what you
want: **Trying to** *bribe*
**someone to let you win
is not a fair way to play
a game.**

bron·co·bust·er
[brong′kō·bus′tər] *n.* A
person who rides wild
horses or bulls: *Bronco-
busters* **sometimes get
hurt when they ride
wild horses.**

bur·row [bûr′ō] *v.* To dig
or hide in a hole: **I watch
my hamster** *burrow* **into
the leaves to make a
warm nest.**

but·ler [but′lər] *n.* A person who works as the
head servant of a house.

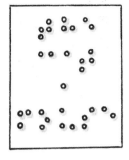

Braille

cal·cu·la·tor
[kal′kyə·lā′tər] *n.* A
small machine used to do
arithmetic problems: **She
used a** *calculator* **to
check her addition and
subtraction.**

ca·noe [kə·nō͞o′] *v.*
ca·noed, ca·noe·ing To
ride in a canoe, which is
a small boat for one or
two people.

cat·a·logue [kat′ə·lôg′ *or*
kat′ə·log′] *n.* A book
that lists things for sale:
**Mr. Cortez orders all his
winter clothes from**
catalogues.

burrow

a	add	o͞o	took
ā	ace	o͞o	pool
â	care	u	up
ä	palm	û	burn
e	end	yo͞o	fuse
ē	equal	oi	oil
i	it	ou	pout
ī	ice	ng	ring
o	odd	th	thin
ō	open	th	this
ô	order	zh	vision

ə = { a in *above*   e in *sicken*
      i in *possible*
      o in *melon*   u in *circus* }

cocoa The people of Mexico gave us our word *cocoa*. Chocolate is made from cocoa beans. Mexicans, who first used chocolate, called it *chocolatl*, their word for "bitter water." Believe it or not, it takes a lot of sugar to make chocolate sweet!

cocoon

compass

conch

cham·pi·on [cham′pē·ən] *n.* A person who wins first place in a contest: **Julie won the spelling bee, so she is now the spelling** *champion* **of our school.** *syn.* winner

chan·de·lier [shan′də·lir′] *n.* A lamp that hangs from the ceiling: **The** *chandelier* **over the table lit up the entire room.**

cho·rus [kôr′əs] *n.* A group of singers.

clat·ter [klat′ər] *v.* **clat·tered, clat·ter·ing** To make a loud crashing or knocking noise: **The dishes** *clattered* **as they broke and fell.**

cock·a·too [kok′ə·tōo′] *n.* A kind of parrot: *Cockatoos* **are beautiful birds with crests of many different colors.**

co·coa [kō′kō] *n.* A hot chocolate drink: **Mrs. Brown gives us a cup of** *cocoa* **whenever we visit.** *syn.* hot chocolate

co·coon [kə·kōon′] *n.* The small home a caterpillar makes while it is changing into a moth: **A caterpillar spins a** *cocoon*, **but a moth comes out of it.**

com·mer·cial [kə·mûr′shəl] *n.* An advertisement on TV or radio for the purpose of selling something: **The makers of cars, cereals, and soaps use TV** *commercials* **to try to get people to buy their products.**

com·pass [kum′pəs *or* kom′pəs] *n.* An instrument that always points to the north, so people can figure out in which direction to go.

com·pete [kəm·pēt′] *v.* To take part in a contest: **Carmen** *competes* **with me every summer to see who can swim across Moby Lake fastest.**

con·cen·trate [kon′sən·trāt′] *v.* To think hard about something or pay very close attention: **Joel is trying hard to** *concentrate* **on his science homework to make sure he does it correctly.**

conch [kongk *or* konch] *n.* A kind of sea animal with a large shell: **We found the beautiful shell of a** *conch* **on the beach today.**

con·ser·va·to·ry
[kən·sûr′və·tôr′ē] *n.* A small greenhouse for growing plants and flowers: **Jim worked in the** *conservatory,* **raising tulips and roses.**

creek [krēk *or* krik] *n.* A small river: **Every summer we waded in the** *creek* **behind our house.** *syns.* stream, brook

crin·kle [kring′kəl] *v.* **crin·kled, crin·kling** To wrinkle or put ridges into: **She** *crinkled* **her nose at the smelly garbage in the alley.**

cu·ri·ous [kyŏŏr′ē·əs] *adj.* Very interested; eager to learn about or do something: **The children were** *curious* **to find out how the story ended.**

dis·ap·point·ed
[dis′ə·point′ed] *adj.* Sad about not getting what was expected.

dol·lop [däl′əp] *n.* A lump or blob of something: **She spread a** *dollop* **of butter on the toast.**

door·step [dôr′step′] *n.* A step leading to an outside door: **I stood on the** *doorstep,* **waiting for someone to come to the door after I knocked.**

dough [dō] *n.* A mix of flour and liquid used to make foods such as bread and muffins: **I added raisins to the** *dough* **before I baked the cookies.**

driz·zle [driz′əl] *n.* Very light rain: **The little bit of** *drizzle* **during our walk didn't get us very wet.** *syn.* mist

crinkle

dollop

easel Our word *easel* came from the Dutch word *ezel,* which means "donkey." Why would a stand made to hold paintings be named after a donkey? Because a donkey is a "beast of burden" used to hold and carry loads, just as an *easel* is.

D

del·i·ca·tes·sen
[del′ə·kə·tes′(ə)n] *n.* A store that sells prepared foods such as sandwiches and salads.

E

ea·sel [ē′zəl] *n.* A frame or stand used to hold the painting an artist is working on.

a	add	ŏŏ	took
ā	ace	ōō	pool
â	care	u	up
ä	palm	û	burn
e	end	yōō	fuse
ē	equal	oi	oil
i	it	ou	pout
ī	ice	ng	ring
o	odd	th	thin
ō	open	th	this
ô	order	zh	vision

ə = { a in *above* e in *sicken*
i in *possible*
o in *melon* u in *circus* }

exhibition

figurehead

fringe

eld·est [el′dist] *n.* The oldest: **Carlos is the *eldest* child in his family because all his brothers and sisters are younger than he is.**

en·er·gy [en′ər·jē] *n.* Power to do something; strength: **I lost all of my *energy* before I finished the race, so I came in last.**

en·ter·tain·ment [en′tər·tān′mənt] *n.* Something performed to interest or give pleasure to an audience: **Movies are my favorite kind of *entertainment*.**

e·vent [i·vent′] *n.* A game or part of a sports show: **My favorite *event* in the Olympics is the ski jumping.**

ex·ag·ger·ate [ig·zaj′ə·rāt′] *v.* **ex·ag·ger·at·ed, ex·ag·ger·at·ing** To make something seem greater or more than it really is: **My brother *exaggerated* when he said he caught a ten-pound fish because it really weighed only five pounds.**

ex·er·cise [ek′sər·sīz′] *n.* Active movement of the body to improve strength or health: **We did *exercises* in gym glass to strengthen our arms.**

ex·hi·bi·tion [ek′sə·bish′ən] *n.* A showing of art: **We liked seeing the paintings at the *exhibition*.** *syn.* exhibit

F

fig·ure·head [fig′yər·hed′] *n.* A carved figure set at the front of a sailing ship: **The old ships in the museum had *figureheads* of different kinds of creatures.**

flut·ter·y [flut′ər·ē] *adj.* Waving back and forth: **Her dress made *fluttery* motions in the breeze.**

frag·ile [fraj′əl] *adj.* Easily broken: **Jean's mother told her to be careful with the *fragile* dishes.**

fringe [frinj] **1** *n.* A trimming of threads hanging from an edge. **2** *v.* To attach or sew on a border of fringe.

frol·ic [frol′ik] *v.*
frol·icked, frol·ick·ing
To play happily about:
**The happy children
were** *frolicking* **in the
first snow of winter.**
syn. romp

G

gig·gle [gig′əl] *v.* To laugh
in a silly way: **All the
children started to** *giggle*
**when Joey dropped his
glasses in the fish tank.**
syn. chuckle

grain [grān] *n.* A tiny bit
or piece of something: **I
couldn't count every**
grain **of sand on this
beach if I had a whole
lifetime to do it.** *syns.*
particle, speck

grand·daugh·ter
[gran(d)′dô′tər] *n.* The
daughter of a person's
son or daughter: **My
four-year-old** *grand-
daughter* **has dark hair
and blue eyes, just like
my son has.**

grump·y [grum′pē] *adj.* In
a bad mood: **I'm** *grumpy*
**because I had a bad day
at school.** *syns.* crabby,
grouchy

H

hand·ker·chief
[hang′kər·chif] *n.* A
square piece of cloth
used to wipe the nose:
**He blew his nose with
his red** *handkerchief.*
syn. hankie

hol·low [hol′ō] *n.* A small
valley: **Ferns grow in the
low ground of the**
hollows.

handkerchief

I

im·i·tate [im′ə·tāt′] *v.*
im·i·tat·ed, im·i·tat·ing
To do something the
same way as someone or
something else: **When we
heard Matt** *imitating*
**Jim's laugh, we thought
Jim was in the room.**

a	add	o͞o	took
ā	ace	o͞o	pool
â	care	u	up
ä	palm	û	burn
e	end	yo͞o	fuse
ē	equal	oi	oil
i	it	ou	pout
ī	ice	ng	ring
o	odd	th	thin
ō	open	th	this
ô	order	zh	vision

ə = { a in *above*   e in *sicken*
i in *possible*
o in *melon*   u in *circus*

jersey The island of Jersey, near the coast of Great Britain, was famous for the soft, knitted woolen cloth made there. About 150 years ago, *jersey* cloth was used to make a new style of shirt. This kind of shirt was called a *jersey*—and it still is.

knapsack

lemming

im·press [im·pres'] *v.* To affect someone's feelings or mind: **Juan hoped that his extra work would** *impress* **his teacher.**

in·vi·ta·tion [in'və·tā'shən] *n.* A message asking someone to come someplace or do something: **He got an** *invitation* **to the birthday party and looked forward to going.**

isle [īl] *n.* A small island: **We paddled our canoe around the** *isle* **in the center of Little Beaver Lake.**

J

jave·lin [jav'(ə·)lin] *n.* A light spear thrown in athletic contests: **Sam won the** *javelin* **contest when he threw the spear farther than anyone else did.**

jer·sey [jûr'zē] *n.* A pullover shirt or sweater: **We knew who the players were by the numbers on their** *jerseys.*

K

knap·sack [nap'sak'] *n.* A bag with shoulder straps, worn on the back: **Joe carried our picnic lunch in his** *knapsack. syn.* backpack

L

la·va·liere [läv'ə·li(ə)r'] *n.* A necklace: **Her gold** *lavaliere* **slipped off her neck during dinner and fell into her tomato soup.**

lem·ming [lem'ing] *n.* A small animal like a rat that lives in the Arctic: *Lemmings* **move from place to place and sometimes drown by rushing blindly into the sea.**

li·brar·i·an [lī·brâr'ē·ən] *n.* A person who works in a library: **Ben asked the** *librarian* **where to find a book about fossils and dinosaurs.**

lu·pine [lo͞o′pin] *n.* A kind of plant related to peas and beans that also has lovely flowers: **We found a blue *lupine* and some other wild flowers growing along the trail.**

mar·a·thon [mar′ə·thon′] *n.* A 26-mile running race: **The young runner trained for months to get ready for the long *marathon*.**

mar·i·gold [mar′ə·gōld′] *n.* A yellow flower: **We planted *marigolds* in our flower garden.**

mar·ma·lade [mär′mə·lād′] *n.* A kind of jam: **The orange *marmalade* Aunt June made tasted good spread on biscuits and toast.**

mast [mast] *n.* A tall pole that holds up a ship's sail: **The storm broke all the ship's *masts*, and the sails crashed into the sea.**

med·i·ca·tion [med′ə·kā′shən] *n.* Medicine; something used to cure an illness: **The doctor gave me some *medication* that cured my sore throat.**

mem·o·rize [mem′ə·rīz′] *v.* **mem·o·rized, mem·o·riz·ing** To learn something by heart: **Mike is so good at *memorizing* songs that he can sing fifty songs without looking at the words.** *syn.* remember

mim·ic [mim′ik] *v.* **mim·icked, mim·ick·ing** To copy or repeat what someone does or says: **The parrot was *mimicking* everything we said so that it sounded like an echo in the room.**

mod·i·fied [mod′ə·fīd] *adj.* Changed slightly: **The *modified* bicycle went faster than it ever had before.**

mur·mur [mûr′mər] *v.* **mur·mured, mur·mur·ing** To make a soft, steady sound: **The brook *murmured* softly in the distance.** *syn.* mumble

lupine

masts

murmur Try saying the syllable *mur* over and over quietly to yourself. What you hear is the sound that is meant by the word *murmur*.

a	add	o͞o	took
ā	ace	o͞o	pool
â	care	u	up
ä	palm	û	burn
e	end	yo͞o	fuse
ē	equal	oi	oil
i	it	ou	pout
ī	ice	ng	ring
o	odd	th	thin
ō	open	th	this
ô	order	zh	vision

ə = { a in *above* e in *sicken*
       i in *possible*
       o in *melon* u in *circus*

nickname Do you have a *nickname*? Long ago in Old English it was called *an ekename*. *Eke* meant "added." So *an ekename* was a name that was added to your real name. After a time, people came to spell it *nickname*.

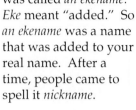

omelette

palette

N

nick·name [nik'nām'] *n.* A short or familiar form of someone's real name: **Alexandria's nickname is Alex.**

nui·sance [n(y)o͞o'səns] *n.* Someone or something that bothers others: **Everyone thought Harold was a nuisance because he cried all the time.**

O

om·e·lette [om'lit *or* om'ə·lit] *n.* An egg dish, often made with cheese: **My dad fixed me a cheese and ham omelette.**

or·chard [ôr'chərd] *n.* A field of trees grown for their fruit or nuts: **We went to the orchard to pick apples.**

out·doors·man [out·dôrz'mən] *n.* A person who enjoys spending time outdoors in nature: **We call Pedro and Luis the family outdoorsmen because they love to fish and hike in the mountains.**

P

pal·ette [pal'it] *n.* A board used by painters to hold and mix different colored paints: **The artist put all the colors he wanted to use for his painting on his palette.**

palm [päm] *n.* The inside of the hand: **We watched the caterpillars crawl along the palms of our hands.**

par·cel [pär'səl] *n.* A package: **I unwrapped the parcel that came in the mail.**

part·ner [pärt'nər] *n.* A person who plays with or helps another person in a game or activity: **Felipe is a good tennis partner because he can hit the shots that Rob has trouble reaching.** *syns.* teammate, companion, buddy

per·form·ance [pər·fôr'məns] *n.* A show, play, or concert in front of an audience: **The audience clapped loudly at the end of the performance.** *syn.* act

pi·o·neer [pī'ə·nir'] *adj.* Having to do with one of the first people to settle in a particular area: **American** *pioneer* **families traveled west in wagons and on horseback to find new homes.**

pis·til [pis'təl] *n.* The part of a flower that produces seeds: **If you open the** *pistil* **of a flower, you will often see the seeds inside.**

plain [plān] *n.* A large area of almost level land without trees: **We could see for miles across the empty** *plains.* *syns.* prairie, field

pol·len [pol'ən] *n.* A powder in plants that helps seeds make new plants: *Pollen* **is sometimes carried from one flower to another flower by bees or butterflies.**

pon·cho [pon'chō] *n.* A rain jacket that is pulled over the head.

prai·rie [prâr'ē] *adj.* Having to do with a large grassy area without trees: *Prairie* **dogs are small animals that live in holes in the ground.**

pre·his·tor·ic [prē'his·tôr'ik] *adj.* From a time very long ago, before written history began: **Dinosaurs were** *prehistoric* **animals.** *syn.* ancient

pro·fes·sion·al [prə·fesh'ən·əl] *adj.* Having to do with a job that requires special training: **An electrician's** *professional* **skill is needed to fix the light switch.**

prompt·ly [prompt'lē] *adv.* Quickly: **We were glad the fire truck arrived** *promptly* **after we called.** *syn.* immediately

prow [prou] *n.* The front end of a boat or ship: **Sailors stood at the** *prows* **of the ships, looking ahead for signs of land.** *syn.* bow

pistil, pollen

prehistoric

R

rec·ol·lec·tion [rek'ə·lek'shən] *n.* Something remembered. *syns.* memory, remembrance

a	add	o͞o	took
ā	ace	o͞o	pool
â	care	u	up
ä	palm	û	burn
e	end	yo͞o	fuse
ē	equal	oi	oil
i	it	ou	pout
ī	ice	ng	ring
o	odd	th	thin
ō	open	th	this
ô	order	zh	vision

ə = { a in *above*   e in *sicken*
      i in *possible*
      o in *melon*   u in *circus* }

329

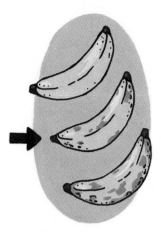

riper

rodeo

scrape

re·cord [rek'ərd] *n.* The best performance in a game or sporting event: **The runner set a world** *record* **in that race.**

rein [rān] *v.* **reined, rein·ing** To pull back or control: **Edward** *reined* **in the ox and stopped plowing at the edge of the field.**

re·tired [ri·tīrd'] *adj.* No longer working: **My mother plans to travel now that she is** *retired.*

rip·er [rīp'ər] *adj.* More ripe; fully grown or ready to eat: **Each day we watched the tomatoes get redder and** *riper.* *syn.* mature

ro·de·o [rō'dē·ō *or* rō·dā'ō] *n.* A contest for people like cowhands to show their skill: **In the** *rodeo,* **he rode the wild horse long enough to win a prize.**

S

sat·is·fac·tion [sat'is·fak'shən] *n.* The feeling of having what you need and want. *syns.* happiness, contentment

schol·ar·ship [skol'ər·ship'] *n.* A prize of money given to students to help them pay for school: **Marilyn's** *scholarship* **will help her pay for her college education.**

sci·en·tist [sī'ən·tist] *n.* A person who finds and studies information about different things: *Scientists* **are trying to figure out why dinosaurs disappeared.**

score [skôr] *n.* The number of points won in a game or contest: **The team with the highest** *score* **wins the game.**

scrape [skrāp] *v.* To take something off by rubbing it with a sharp edge: *Scrape* **the food off the plates before washing them.**

sculpt [skulpt] *v.* To make or shape a statue: **The artist likes to** *sculpt* **the shapes of faces in clay.** *syn.* form

set·tler [set'lər] *n.* Someone who comes to live in a new area: **The early American** *settlers* **came mainly from Europe to this land.**

shiv·er [shiv'ər] *v.* To shake because of feeling cold or afraid. *syn.* tremble

short·en·ing [shôr'tən·ing] *n.* Butter or oil used in cooking: **Mom added *shortening* to the cake batter.**

shriek [shrēk] *v.* **shrieked, shriek·ing** To scream: **We couldn't sleep last night because the sick baby kept *shrieking*.** *syns.* yelp, yell

side·line [sīd'līn'] *n.* A boundary line at the side of a sports field or court: **The fans stood on the *sideline* of the football field.**

skil·let [skil'it] *n.* A frying pan.

speck·led [spek'əld] *adj.* Marked with small dots. *syn.* freckled

splin·ter [splin'tər] *n.* A thin piece of wood split off from a larger piece: ***Splinters* from the wood got in my fingers.**

sport [spôrt] *n.* A game or an athletic contest.

sports·man·ship [spôrts'mən·ship'] *n.* Fairness in playing games or sports.

stern·ly [stûrn'lē] *adv.* Firmly; strictly: **The girl spoke to her brother so *sternly* that the boy began to cry.** *syn.* harshly

stretch [strech] *v.* To pull out or loosen the body's muscles: **My coach told me to *stretch* my arms and legs before every swimming race.**

stumped [stumpt] *adj. informal* Confused or without an answer: **The math problem was so difficult even our teacher was *stumped*.**

sub·way [sub'wā'] *n.* An underground train.

T

ter·race [ter'is] *n.* A paved area for sitting outside: **Tom asked his mother if he could eat his dinner outside on the *terrace*.** *syn.* patio

ther·mos [thûr'məs] *n.* A bottle for keeping liquids hot or cold for several hours.

sport Our word *sport* goes back to ancient Latin roots. *Dis-* is a prefix meaning "away from." *Portare* means "to carry." People joined these roots to make the word *disport*, meaning "to carry away from" work or worry. Later, it was shortened to *sport*.

stretch

a	add	o͞o	took
ā	ace	o͞o	pool
â	care	u	up
ä	palm	û	burn
e	end	yo͞o	fuse
ē	equal	oi	oil
i	it	ou	pout
ī	ice	ng	ring
o	odd	th	thin
ō	open	th	this
ô	order	zh	vision

ə = { a in *above*   e in *sicken*
 i in *possible*
 o in *melon*   u in *circus* }

tropical

wilderness

thread [thred] *n.* A very thin string of cloth: **He used cotton** *thread* **to sew a tear in the old plaid shirt.**

tin·kling [ting'kling] *adj.* Sounding soft and like a small bell.

track [trak] *adj.* Having to do with running races and jumping contests: **At the** *track* **meet last Thursday, she won the 200-meter run.**

tran·quil [trang'kwil *or* tran'kwil] *adj.* Calm and quiet: **We easily rowed the boat across the** *tran-quil* **lake.** *syn.* peaceful

trop·i·cal [trop'i·kəl] *adj.* Like or related to a jungle or warm climate: **We enjoyed the warm weather and delicious fruit on the** *tropical* **island.**

U

u·ten·sil [yo͞o·ten'səl] *n.* A tool used to do or make something: **We keep our gardening** *utensils* **in the garage.**

V

vac·u·um [vak'yo͞o(·ə)m] *n.* A kind of bottle that keeps liquids hot or cold: **Maria kept the ice water in a tightly closed** *vacuum* **bottle to keep it cold.**

W

wharf [(h)wôrf] *n., pl.* **wharves** or **wharfs** A dock along a shore, where boats wait to load or unload: **The fishermen steered their boats toward the** *wharves* **to unload the day's catch.**

wil·der·ness [wil'dər·nis] *n.* An area where people have not settled: **The family happily hiked and camped in the** *wilderness* **for three weeks.** *syn.* outdoors

INDEX OF
TITLES AND AUTHORS

Page numbers in light print refer to information about the author.

Acknowledgments continued

Marian Reiner, on behalf of Myra Cohn Livingston: Untitled riddle (Retitled: "Closed, I Am a Mystery") from *My Head Is Red and Other Riddle Rhymes* by Myra Cohn Livingston. Text copyright © 1990 by Myra Cohn Livingston. Published by Holiday House.

Marian Reiner, on behalf of Lillian Morrison: "Would You Like" by Lillian Morrison. Text copyright © 1983 by Lillian Morrison.

Scholastic, Inc.: From *A Seed Is a Promise* by Claire Merrill. Text copyright © 1973 by Claire Merrill.

Sports Illustrated for Kids: "Wonder Woman" by Joy Duckett Cain from *Sports Illustrated for Kids*, March 1990. Text copyright © 1990 by The Time Inc. Magazine Company.

Tumbledown Editions: "Hello Book!" by N. M. Bodecker. Text copyright © 1974 by N. M. Bodecker; text copyright © 1990 by Tumbledown Editions. Originally published by the Children's Book Council, Inc.

Viking Penguin, a division of Penguin Books USA Inc.: Miss Rumphius by Barbara Cooney. Copyright © 1982 by Barbara Cooney Porter. Cover illustration by Barbara Cooney from *Ox-Cart Man* by Donald Hall. Illustration copyright © 1979 by Barbara Cooney Porter.

Peter Weevers: Cover illustration by Peter Weevers from *The Hare and the Tortoise* by Caroline Castle. Illustration copyright © 1985 by Peter Weevers. Published by Dial Books.

Handwriting models in this program have been used with permission of the publisher, Zaner-Bloser, Inc., Columbus, OH.

Photograph Credits

Key: (t) top, (b) bottom, (l) left, (r) right, (c) center.

UNIT 1

14, HBJ/Maria Paraskevas; 16–17, HBJ Photo; 31, Douglas Merriam; 38–39, HBJ Photo; 56–71, HBJ; 72(t), Courtesy *Sun Newspapers*; 72(b), Courtesy *English Forward*; 72–73 (background), HBJ Photo; 73(t), Courtesy Johanna Hurwitz; 73(b), Courtesy Johanna Hurwitz; 74–75, HBJ/Britt Runion; 78, HBJ/Britt Runion; 80(l), Peter Miller/Sports Illustrated; 80–81, Mike Powell/ Allsport; 81(r), Allsport; 82, Joe McNally/Sygma; 83, David Klutha/ Sports Illustrated; 84(l), Tony Duffy/Allsport; 84(r), Allsport; 85, Scott Weersing/Allsport; 86(l), Tony Duffy/Allsport; 86(r), Peter Read Miller/Sports Illustrated; 87(l), Tony Duffy/Allsport; 87(r), Peter Read Miller/Sports Illustrated; 88, Alan Levenson; 112(t), William Campbell for *Time;* 113(t), William Campbell.

UNIT 2

118–119, HBJ/Debi Harbin; 122, HBJ Photo; 134, Courtesy Morrow Publishers; 178–179, HBJ/Britt Runion; 205, Courtesy Mildred Pitts Walter; 208(t), Reuters/Bettmann; 209(t), Nina Berman/Sipa Press; 209(c), Nina Berman/Sipa Press.

UNIT 3

214–215, HBJ/Maria Paraskevas; 216, HBJ Photo; 256–257, HBJ/ Maria Paraskevas; 258, HBJ Photo; 273(background), HBJ Photo; 273(l), Thomas Dyer; 273(r), Jason Stemple; 274, Jason Stemple; 276–277, HBJ/Maria Paraskevas; 278, HBJ/Maria Paraskevas; 280, HBJ/Maria Paraskevas; 282, HBJ Photo; 283, HBJ Photo; 293, HBJ/Robert Foothorap for Black Star; 295, HBJ/Britt Runion; 296, HBJ/Maria Paraskevas; 298(t), Courtesy Paul Sierra; 298(b), Robert Berman Gallery; 310–311, HBJ/Maria Paraskevas; 320, Gail Denham/PP/FA; 326, Gail Denham/PP/FA; 327, Jay King/PP/FA; 330, John P. Kelly/Image Bank; 331, ZAO Productions/Image Bank; 332(t), Elyse Lewin/Image Bank; 332(b), Grant V. Faint/Image Bank.

Illustration Credits

Key: (t) top, (b) bottom, (l) left, (r) right, (c) center.

Table of Contents Art

Tina Holdcroft, 4 (bl), 6 (tl); Burton Morris, 4–5(c), 7(tr), 8(bl); Tim Raglin, 4(tl), 5(br), 6–7(c), 8(tl); Peggy Tagel, 5(tr), 7(br), 9(tr), 9(br).

Unit Opening Patterns

Dan Thoner

Bookshelf Art

Alex Boies, 212–213; Callie Buytler, 116–117; Armen Kojoytian, 12–13.

Theme Opening Art

Roger Chandler, 78–79; Susan Nees, 140–141; Tim Raglin, 54–55; Tracy Sabin, 256–257; Valerie Sinclair, 280–281.

Theme Closing Art

Seymour Chwast, 255; Regan Dunnick, 207; Cameron Eagle, 139; Peter Horjus, 53; Dave Jonason, 297; Paul Meisel, 65, 77, 177; Lynn Tanaka, 111; Gregg Valley, 279.

Connections Art

David Diaz, 112–113, 208–209; Clarence Porter, 298–299.

Selection Art

Karen Barber, 76; Barbara Cooney, 16–30; Louis Darling, 120, 121, 135; Brian Deines, 180–205; Tomie dePaola, 216–237, 238, 239; Jane Dyer, 258–275; Andrea Eberbach, 32–37, 295, 296; Peggy Fortnum, 240–254; Dan Hobbs, 90–107; Steven Kellogg, 38–52; Laura C. Kelly, 162–176; Roberta Ludlow, 160, 161; Merle Nacht, 276, 277; Allen Say, 282–292, 294; Greg Shed, 142–159; Jackie Snider, 206; Michael Stiernagle, 278; Alan Tiegreen, 122–133, 136, 138; Karen Visser, 108–110.